100 E DESIGN PRINCIPLES

DESIGN MEDIA PUBLISHING LIMITED

Editor's Words

The design process of home interior space integrates rational thinking and emotional thinking, the two different modes of thinking, which lead to the diversification of the final result. The designer creates numerous space images in the process of adhering to the original concept and dealing with various incompatible contradictions.

The book divides home interior design into five modules, namely, space design, structural design, interface design, decorative design and the design of special areas. Meanwhile, one hundred homologous subjects derive further from all the five modules, which give detailed description of the problems that may be confronted and need to be taken into careful consideration in home interior design in the manner of case show.

The book contains such contents as theoretical summaries, drawing analyses, image demonstration and image analyses. In the analyses of the drawings, the corresponding plans are also provided in accordance with the logical relations between the different interior functional areas besides the plane layout drawings of the relative floors. Moreover, the visual directions are indicated by the directional arrows in correspondence to each photo. The meticulous way of presentation can not only make the readers know clearly and thoroughly the constituents of the successful design cases, but provide the designers with a transitional experience from the plane to the space. Moreover, all the text analyses come from the explanation of the designer of each project. The sentiments of excitement and puzzlement experienced by the designers in the design process can easily be perceived from these pellucid words.

The book aims to provide the relevant designers with a reference to the innovative inspiration, an editing purpose demonstrated from its professional, systematic, intuitive and legible qualities. We can find the sequence of ideas of home space design belonging to our era through the profound analysis of each case so as to reflect on the design motivation and significance behind the numerous visual presentations.

Contents

INTERFACE DESIGN PRINCIPLES

Contents

DESIGN PRINCIPLES OF SPECIAL AREAS

BEGINNING

1 Conception of residential interior design

The approach of home design is the comprehensive reflection of the comprehension and conception of the site conditions in the designers' mind, the results of which will eventually be demonstrated through visual images. The so-called visual images are the innovative grasp of the site conditions, which embodies the designers' imagination, creativity and their understanding of the aesthetic concepts, rather than the mechanical duplication of perceptual materials. Home design is the designing process of the four-dimensional space, therefore the sense of beauty of home design is reflected in the whole space and it is necessary for the designers to apprehend according to the state of motion of different spaces.

In this case, the designer is required by the clients to retain the historical construction features of the original building and use their art collections as the main decorative elements of the interior space.

Project name: Capps Residence **Completion date:** 2008 **Location:** Texas, USA **Designer:** Poteet Architects, San Antonio, Texas **Photographer:** Ryann Ford **Area:** 305 sqm

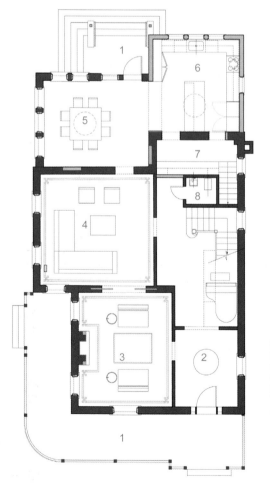

1. Porch
2. Parlour
3. Sitting
4. Living
5. Dining
6. Kitchen
7. Butler's pantry
8. Powder room

First Floor Plan

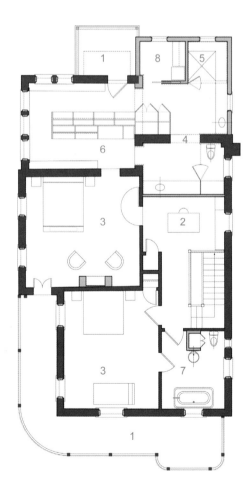

1. Porch
2. Office
3. Bedroom
4. Master bath
5. Master shower
6. Closet
7. Guest bath
8. Utility

Second Floor Plan

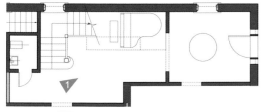

Parlour+Butler's Pantry+Powder Room Plan

1. Client engaged designer to tailor the house to his needs, without sacrificing the historic character its prominent site demanded. Bold colour surprises are interjected at intervals to keep the white palette fresh: the robin's egg blue in the foyer reflects the owners' love of colour and visual sense of humour
2. Client's art collection is an international showcase
3. The design team found sources from all over the world to incorporate into the home's design

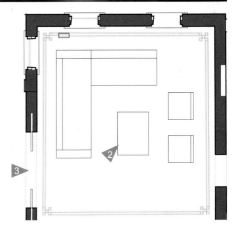

Living Room Plan

1. The interior of the home was transformed to support the lifestyle of the new owners

2. The kitchen is sheathed in honed carrara marble, including open shelves which span the banks of windows. The storage on the kitchen is extended by a butler's pantry which is tucked into the basement access of the old residence

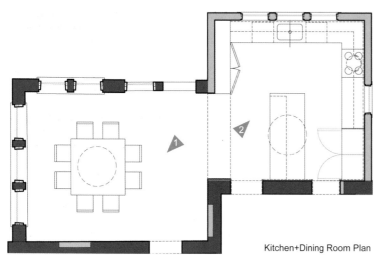

Kitchen+Dining Room Plan

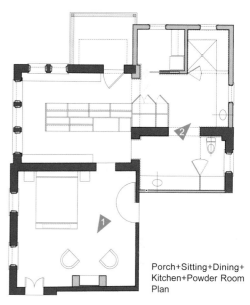

Porch+Sitting+Dining+
Kitchen+Powder Room
Plan

1. Museum-quality lighting is installed throughout controlled by a "smart house" system which also operates the audio visual and security systems

2. In the master closet and bath, the designers had the full opportunity to express the personality of the owners. The master closet and bath are merged into one flowing space dominated by the black closet island and the large glass-tiled steam shower in four colours of blue

3. Clients are avid collectors of contemporary art and open their home for entertaining and large events on a regular basis. The interior design supports the passion by unifying the restored plaster walls in white and the floors in ebony

2 Pay equal attention to form and function

The foothold of home design is to provide people with a comfortable and convenient living environment. During the programming process, the designer continually deliberates and transforms between different concepts, both closed and flowing, public and private, setting about from the use of the interior space. So to speak, the functional layout of home design mainly focuses on studying the relationship between the circulation and the utilisation of space involving such space-time elements as form and structure, distance, location and scale. However, human heings, as the senior animals, have their unique demands not only for the physical environment of the interior space but also for the visual delight. In this way, the designer, on one hand, should make sure the rational function partition, and on the other hand, make a unified arrangement of the interface and the formal beauty of space configuration.

In this case, the designer devises a flowing image of wall that effectively connects different spaces, satisfying the rationality of function deployment and offering the client a rich visual experience.

Project name: Living Pod **Completion date:** 2008 **Location:** Hong Kong, China **Designer:** Mr. Joey Ho **Other Designer:** Ms. Bobo Tsui **Photographer:** Mr. Graham Uden, Mr. Ray Lau **Area:** 204 sqm

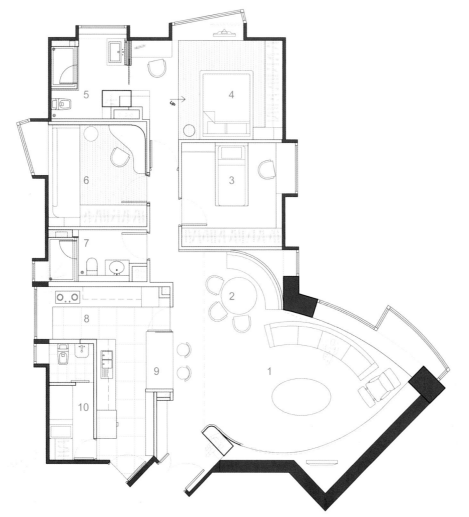

Master Plan

1. Living area
2. Dining area
3. Bedroom B
4. Bedroom A
5. Bathroom
6. Study room
7. Bathroom
8. Kitchen
9. Bar
10. Maid's room

1. The designer builds a streamlined wall feature and lets it wrap around the living space from dining to living area, and continue all the way down to the foyer

2. This innovative framework conjures up a sense of enclosure and creates a new spatial relationship for the interior, which helps to create an open and cohesive spatial relationship

3. Despite its prime location at the busy CBD, the design succeeds in bringing nature in a contemporary setting by wrapping all the functional spaces via a clean-cut expression, letting different activities proceed and overlap in a natural and fluid manner

4. In contrast to the existing angular shape of the apartment, curvy shape is used as the backbone of the interior structure

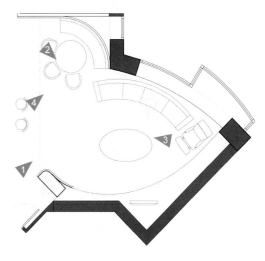

Entrance+Living+Dining Room Plan

Bar Plan

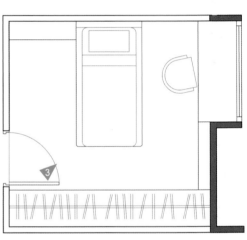

Bedroom B Plan

1. Located at the metropolitan centre of Hong Kong, this mid-level apartment presents a new sensation of living that celebrates life and nature

2. Innovative elements like the leisurely bathroom with a floor-to-ceiling glass wall with a beach picture printed on it help bringing the sense of nature into the interior space and constructing a personal retreat that is detached from the city

3. In this comfortable living pod, the designer has incorporated a number of interesting settings to represent the modern lifestyle of the owner, while at the same time embody its relation with nature

1. The blue shade background suggests the natural atmosphere of the space

2. The clean and simple closet under the reflection of the lighting and mirror gives a sense of lightness

3. The materials of glass and mirror have greatly weakened the sense of heaviness of the wall

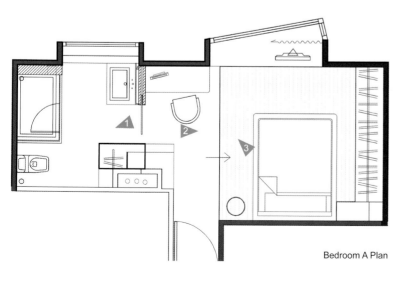

Bedroom A Plan

3 From plane to space

It is in line with the layout procedure and logic that home design begins with layout planning. The layout planning here includes the two-dimensional wall space in the drawings, the floor and the top space. On meditating these two-dimensional images, there will appear a real and flowing space image in the designer's mind. Such comprehensive illusion, definitely, may change by any possibilities. However, this kind of conversion process will go with the whole designing process. The ways of spatial thinking of the two dimensions comprise the visual perception of the varied functional areas from different viewpoints and the visual effect of duplication of the furnishing items and the interface, which is the premise to guarantee the spatial integrity and unity.

In this case, the designer creates a simple spatial ambience by mainly selecting the minimalism style furniture matched with the simple interface design.

Project name: First Crescent **Completion date:** 2007 **Location:** Camps Bay, South Africa **Architects:** SAOTA (Stefan Antoni Olmesdahl Truen Architects) - Stefan Antoni, Philip Olmesdahl, Tamaryn Hammond **Interior Design:** Antoni Associates – Mark Rielly, Ashleigh Gilmour **Photographer:** Wieland Gleich & Karl Beath **Area:** 676 sqm

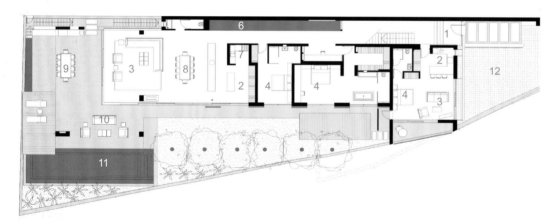

Ground Floor Plan

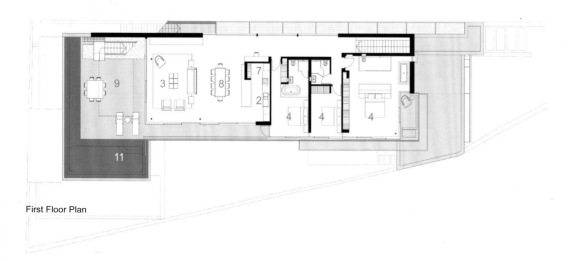

First Floor Plan

1. Entrance
2. Kitchen
3. Lounge
4. Bedroom
5. Study
6. Pond
7. Scullery
8. Dining room
9. Terrace dining
10. Terrace lounge
11. Pool
12. Driveway

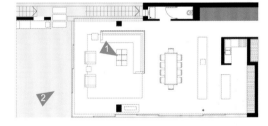

Lounge Plan

1. Designers believe that the most successful living spaces are uncluttered, refined and have a great directness which complements the casual lifestyle of the clients

2. The design speaks of a lifestyle, one of entertaining for all seasons with the lines between external and internal being deliberately blurred. Glazing is always full height with ceilings at 3 metres above the finished floor levels

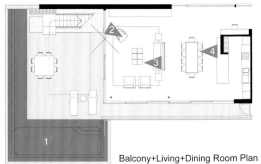

Balcony+Living+Dining Room Plan

1. The terraces adjacent to the living areas are large, each with their own swimming pools and barbeque, rendering them ideal for entertaining

2. Even though the furniture is simple and minimal, warmth was introduced through textured fabrics and surface finishes. The colour palette is neutral (soft greys and charcoals) with flashes of bright colour being introduced through accent pieces

3. Aluminium was kept light and understated and the eye is drawn beyond the space and always to the distant view. Each room opens out externally and it is the shape of the site which really defines the exterior spaces

4. The sliding doors of the living areas open away from each other ensuring that internal living effortlessly spills out onto the terraces without interruption. Colours and the choice of materials also played a vital role with large elegant porcelain floor tiles being used throughout

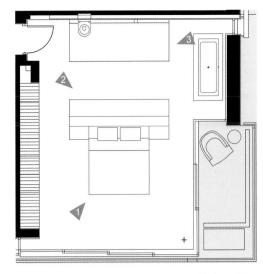

Bedroom Plan

1. The bedrooms are situated where the site is at its narrowest. "Zen" type gardens, timber decks and natural materials define these smaller areas as being ideal for quiet contemplation

2. Due to the linearity of the site it made sense to integrate the bedrooms and bathrooms as each was more spacious with its own natural light. If enclosed, the bathrooms would have been very tight and would have relied entirely on mechanical ventilation and artificial lighting

3. "Elegance" was a priority, and therefore SAOTA opted to have them custom-made. Each basin plays off the same theme but is totally unique and designed specifically to suite the space in which it is installed

4 The creation of space ambience

The presentation of the interior space's atmosphere is the visual experience of the man's senses about the corporeal substance and virtual space. The corporeal substance is composed with the enclosure interface, building structure, furnishings and other three-dimensional forms, whose various shapes and matched colours as well as contrasted materials could visually express the idea of the designer and the space style. Virtual space is formed by enclosing the corporeal substance, which plays important role in space's size, tone, actual situation as well as ambience. The ambience of space is the essence of home design and also the goal that the designer is seeking for.

In this case, the designers employ flexible design techniques to divide the space perfectly and have created continuous but also private areas; from the perspective of detailed design, designers have retained the original building components and elements and matched with the handcrafted furnishings, giving the space a sense of texture and tactility.

Project name: Greene Street Loft **Completion date:** 2008 **Location:** New York, USA **Designer:** Slade Architecture **Photographer:** Jordi Miralles **Area:** 300 sqm

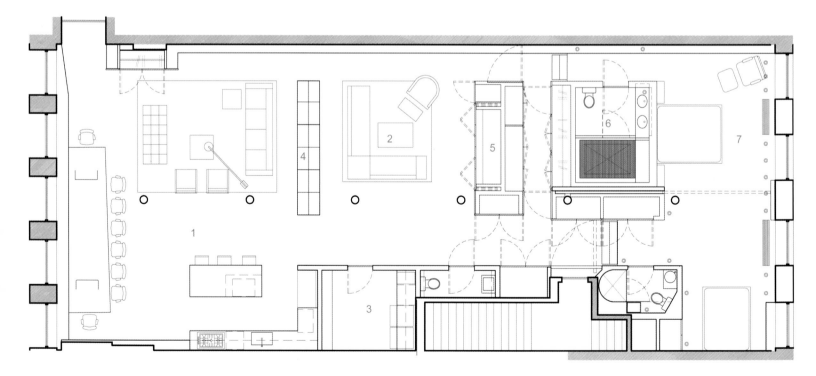

Master Plan

1. Living room and kitchen
2. Study
3. Sleeping loft
4. Aluminium shelf
5. Closet
6. Bathroom
7. Bedroom

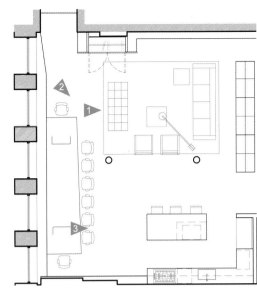

Living+Dining+Kichen Plan

1. The first volume is an aluminium bookcase designed to hold the owner's collection of traditional Korean trunks. The bookcase separates the living, dining and kitchen areas from the study. The side of the bookcase facing the living room is deep and is designed specifically to house the trunk collection

2. Designer selected all of the furniture and finishes and designed a custom silk rug in the living room that fades from blue at the edges to silver in the centre. The custom table designed out of a single, 19' long and 48" wide, slice of Mokore is the focal point for parties and entertaining. It seats about twenty people and runs the length of the east-facing windows

3. The kitchen island is cladded in acrylic and the top is marble, supported by a concealed steel structure

4. The upper cabinet doors in the kitchen are solid acrylic (light blocks). The countertop is marble and matches the marble on the steps up to the bedroom. The lower cabinets are stainless steel

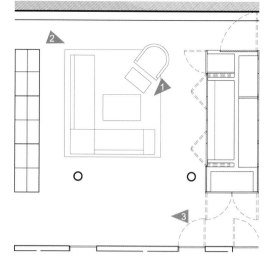

Study Room Plan

1. The second volume contains a built-in desk area facing the study and a closet on the other side

2. Two hidden doors allow the corridor between this volume and the third volume (the walk-in closet) to be closed off

3. Three eight-foot-tall freestanding volumes arranged down the centre of the existing space define the different programme areas and provide a continuous view through the entire depth of the apartment and function as corridors linking the different areas of the apartment

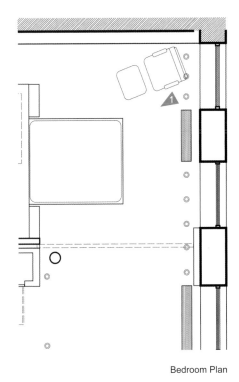

Bedroom Plan

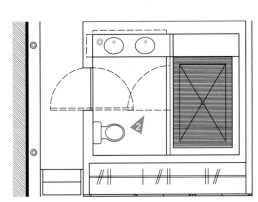

Bathroom Plan

1. The bedrooms and bathrooms are lifted on a rough stone platform about 16" above the rest of the floor. The headboard in the master bedroom is a teak slat wall. Bright orange lacquer shelves inserted into the slats can be rearranged by the owner as needed

2. The masterbath has a large convertible tub/shower. The "his and hers" shower has a teak slat floor that can be removed to reveal a large soaking bathtub

SPACE DESIGN PRINCIPLES

5 Closure and enclosure

A quiet and tranquil spatial ambience can be created by closing and connecting various parts of the home space. This kind of spatial characteristic of the interior space including the enclosed interfaces possesses a strong definition. The space maintains its introversion and privacy as well as the symmetrical centrality with a strong sense of territoriality. The proportion and scale between the enclosed interface and the decorative furnishings keep a highly coordinate and unified relationship.

In this case, the designer successfully designs a spatial ambience which enjoys the highly symmetrical centrality with a strong sense of territoriality. The size comparison of the home furnishing items and its spatial environment coordinate with each other, which makes the spatial image more abundant and graceful. A finishing touch goes to the handling of the entrance hallway, by which the designer makes the small space broader by the collocation of coordinate ratios and scales.

Project name: Apartment No.10 **Completion date:** 2010 **Location:** Chengdu, China **Designer:** MoHen Design International **Photographer:** MoHen Design International

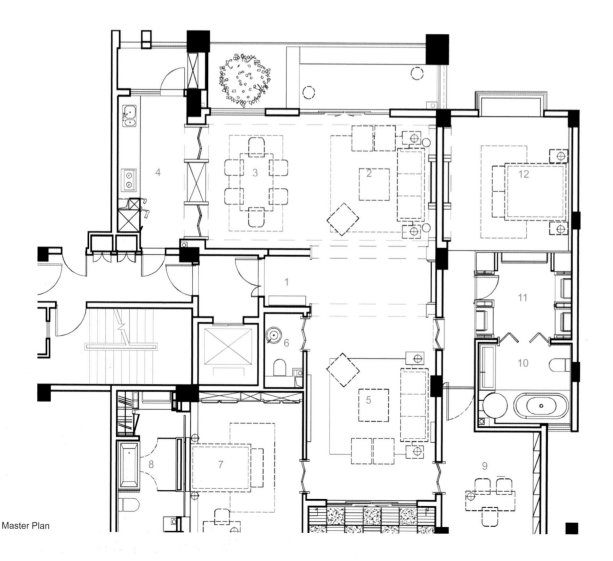

Master Plan

1. Foyer
2. Family room
3. Dining room
4. Kitchen
5. Living room
6. Powder room
7. Guest bedroom
8. Guest bath
9. Study room
10. Master bath
11. Dressing room
12. Master bedroom

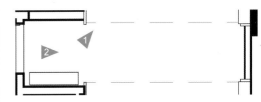

Foyer Plan

1. The reflection effect of the mirror has broken the closed foyer and the multiple reflections give the limited space a sense of infinite visual illusion

2 The narrow entrance area to the foyer limits the range of sight, and the reflection effect of the top has strengthened the sense of depth

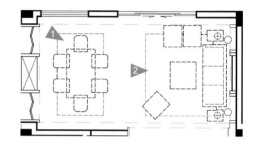

Famliy Room+Dining Room Plan

Living Room Plan

1. The decorative interface has weakened the sense of enclosure and enriched the limited dining space with various visual changes. The design of ceiling strengthens the closed space and naturally links different functional areas together

2. Checkerboard carpet adds the closed living space a different orderly visual experience

3. The bouncing shape of the top and wall enhances the sense of depth; the texture and colour of the sofa and floor inject the closed space a sense of weight

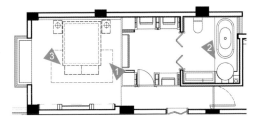

Master Bath+Dressing Room+ Master Bedroom Plan

1. The textures of the curtain and background echo each other, and have weakened the sense of enclosure caused by the interface

2. Bar mosaic has integrated the floor and wall effectively and created a rich visual experience

3. The symmetrical wall decoration makes the narrow bedroom wall be more flexible

6 Openness and dynamic

The openness of the interior space together with the fluid forms could enhance the communication between the inside environment and that of outside, and can also easily create a moving visual effect of the four-dimensional space. This space features with the less integrity of the enclosure interfaces; part of which remain the open state and strong extraversion but less restriction and could naturally interact with nature and surrounding environment; the transformation of the enclosure interface is distinctive and the patterns give a sense of dynamic.

In this case, the designers chose a linear texture interface and organically linked the swimming pool, gardens and public space together, to achieve the visual effect that sceneries vary with the changing view-points.

Project name: 55 Blair Road **Completion date:** 2009 **Location:** Singapore City, Singapore **Designer:** Ong&Ong Pte Ltd **Photographer:** Derek Swalwell **Area:** 288 sqm **Awarded:** ArchDaily Building of the Year Award (Refurbishment)

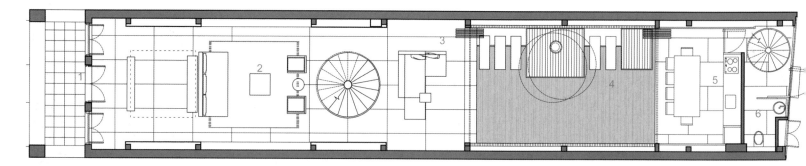

1. Entrance
2. Living
3. Bedroom
4. Landscape
5. Dining
6. Bathroom

First Floor Plan

Section Plan

1. Glazed walls separate the rest of the first floor from the outdoor pool and frangipani garden in the middle of the courtyard

2. When both glazed partitions are open, the first floor transforms into a single large space, achieving diversity of space with a lounge, dining area and poolside

3. Absence of walls is ideal for cross-ventilation between the various spaces inside the house – a natural cooling system overcomes Singapore's humidity

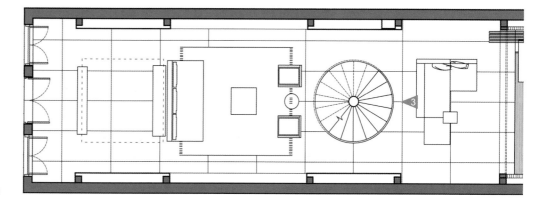

Entrance+Living Plan

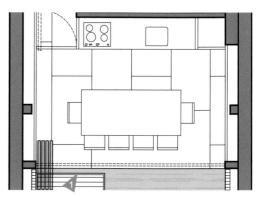

Dining Plan

1. The kitchen was finished in a seamless aluminium cladding, adding a touch of refinement

2. The master bedroom on the second floor also has an en suite bathroom – a glazed box that protrudes out and over the pool area

3. This modern intervention plays with conventional ideas of space, and is a refreshing feature of the house

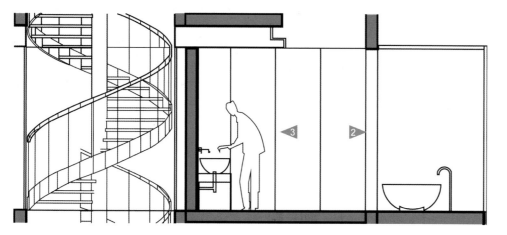

Bathroom Section

1. The plan of the master bedroom space is true to the axial layout of the house, and symmetrical bookshelves line the walls that lead to the study area

2. To overcome the constraint of maintaining the height of the second floor a new mezzanine space was created to accommodate an additional guest bedroom in the attic space

3. A home automation system controls the lighting on the main building, creating a variety of moods and settings, with special care to minimise energy. Another unique feature of the master bedroom is the viewing well in the middle of the room that provides a window of sorts to the second floor

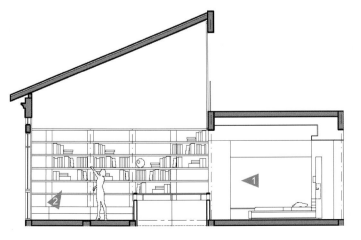

Second Floor Section

7 Virtual space

Being the most enchanting one among all types of interior space, the virtuality of the home space creates a spatial environment that meets the functional and aesthetic requirements through its own substantive characteristics and moreover produces an artistic conception. Rather than being restricted to the elements that depend on the interfacial enclosure, this spatial type divides the space by the formal and structural implications and men's visual imagination. The most remarkable characteristics can be concluded as follows: dividing the space symbolically so as to form the visual transparency as well as maintain to the limit the blending and continuous spatial attribute; boasting the flowing and instructive features of the linear space; generating the visual imagination by means of building structure and decorative elements. The virtuality of the interior space deduces various kinds of space on the basis of the elements such as interior structures, materials, interfaces and modellings.

In this case, the designer creates the Zen style spatial ambience through the abstract technique of spatial modelling and the concise colour matching. Just as the designer says, this is a place where you can meditate and fantasise earnestly.

Project name: Moliner House **Completion date:** 2008 **Location:** Zaragoza, Spain **Designer:** Alberto Campo Baeza **Photographer:** Javier Callejas **Area:** 216 sqm

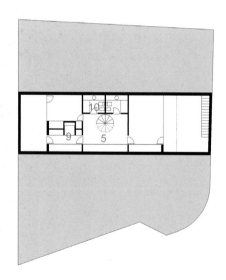

B1 Plan

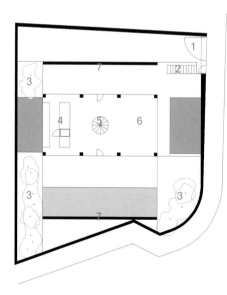

First Floor Plan

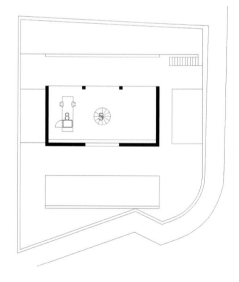

Second Floor Plan

1. Entrance
2. Stairs
3. Garden
4. Dining
5. Atrium stairs
6. Living
7. Walls
8. Sanctum
9. Cabin
10. Bedroom

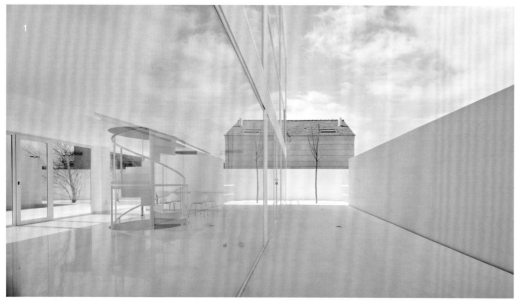

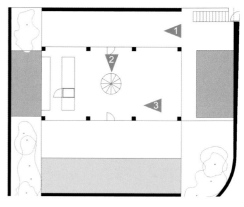

First Floor Plan

1. Architects raised high walls to create a box open to the sky, like a nude, metaphysical garden with concrete walls and floor. To create an interior world, the designers dug into the ground to plant leafy trees

2. For living, the garden with southern light-sunlight. A space that is all garden, with transparent walls that bring together inside and outside

3. The garden is enclosed by concrete walls, an antiseptic interior that ventures into the outdoors blurring the line between the two. Light from the north pours through the glazed walls in the interior cube, reflecting from the white concrete floors and bouncing on the "galeria white" walls

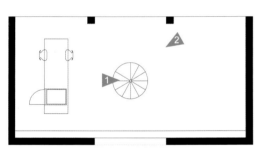

Second Floor Plan

1. The library: a place for dreaming. Dazzling whiteness and translucent glass walls reflect light in all its manifestations. Does the space feel too abstract? Some people like to live with a precise number of elements and a lot of emotions. Could it be that simple geometry should follow a passionate way of being?

2. For dreaming, the designers created a cloud at the highest point. A library constructed with high walls of light diffused through large translucent glass. With northern light for reading and writing, thinking and feeling

8 The form of space

The form of the home space mainly refers to space and the scale and the proportion of the enclosure interface. People always use the habitual or familiar scale concept to measure the size of interior space, so different scales and proportion will produce various visual results. In addition, the scale and the proportion of enclosure interface also obviously affect people's feeling, for the reason that even though people are walking in the interior space, their visual experiences are mainly from the enclosed interface. Under the premise of meeting the spatial scale and proportion, the enclosure interface design also needs to take account of the area, line, length and width, material and other factors so as to provide a comfortable and attractive interior environment.

In this case, the overall space is transformed by opening up two apartments. The designer aims to create a luxurious space, and make the layout full of diversity. In this space, the collocation of the classical and modern elements helps completely conveying the designer's idea.

Project name: Bond Street Loft **Completion date:** 2010 **Location:** New York, USA **Designer:** NEMA Workshop **Photographer:** David Joseph **Area:** 288 sqm

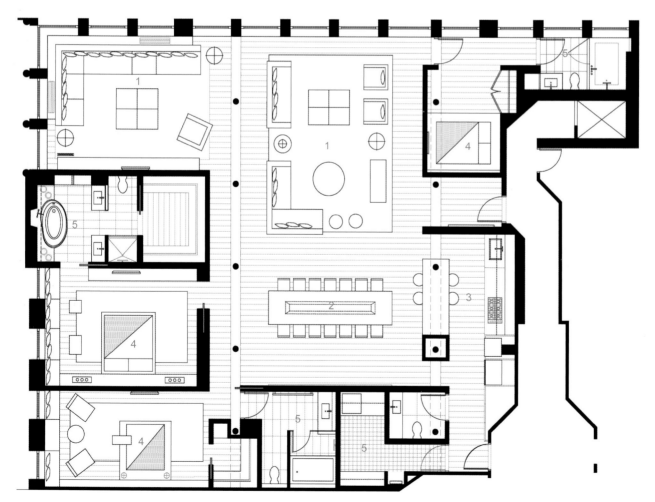

1. Living room
2. Dining area
3. Kitchen
4. Bedroom
5. Bathroom

Master Plan

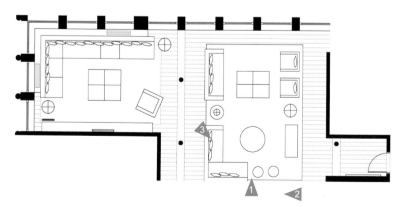

1. The 3,400 square feet loft space joins two apartments in a historical building with an open floor plan which is both seamless and spacious. The concept was to create an environment which was luxurious in materials yet informal in layout

2. The exhibits create a supremely comfortable environment infused with an atmosphere of effortless cool

3. The main living space contains the kitchen, the dining area, the living space and the library. The areas are distinct but they bleed together seamlessly in the open floor plan

Living Room Plan

1. The project combines traditional architectural elements, such as the pillars, with modern elements, which gives people the feeling of time travel

2. Dining area

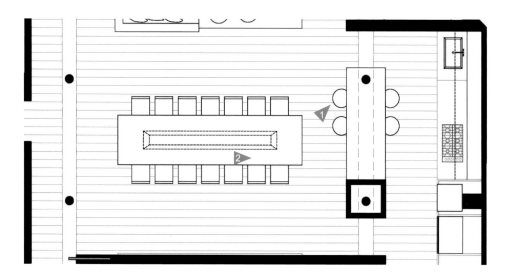

Dining Area+Kitchen Plan

1. Master bathroom
2. Guest bathroom

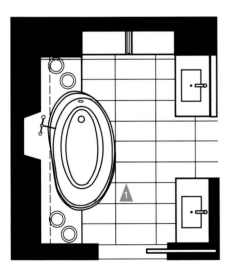

Master Bathroom Plan

9 Space design and detailed structure

The design of the home interior space mainly refers to the interfaces of space and enclosure which mostly constitute human's visual impression. While it is the detailed structure that could present the quality of space and link human with the interior space together, providing visual basis for people to better experience the atmosphere of space. The detailed structure contains original structure components and many decorative elements, among which materials, craftship and scale as well as proportion of the interface have great influence on conveying the theme of the overall space.

In this case, the fine wood furniture and laser-cut Moroccan style bronze stair railing as well as other detail elements inject the room a sense of elegance and texture.

Project name: Murray Hill Townhouse **Completion date:** 2009 **Location:** New York City, USA **Designer:** SPG Architects **Photographer:** Daniel Levin **Area:** 700 sqm

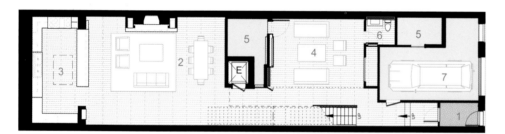

1. Entry
2. Living/dining
3. Kitchen
4. Media room
5. Mechanical
6. Bathroom
7. Garage
8. Master bedroom
9. Dressing room
10. Master bathroom
E =Elevator

First Floor Plan

Second Floor Plan

1. Entry
2. Living/dining
3. Kitchen
4. Master bedroom
5. Billiards room
6. Study terrace
7. Bathroom
8. Sunroom
9. Bathrm/sauna
10. Penthouse terrace
11. Hot tub

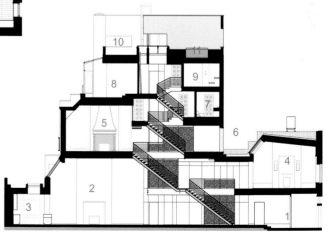

Section Plan

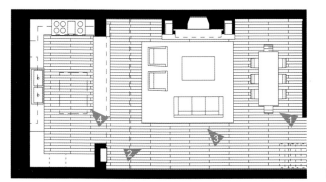

Dining+Living+Kitchen Plan

1. Both the space and the furnishings are commodious and clean-lined with a palette of browns, blues and golds that compliment the architecture

2. The living area, as well as the entire house, is comfortable yet luxuriously modern. The walnut panelling on the wall serves many purposes. It provides a focal point for the large double-height living space and defines the dining area

3. With just enough accessories and incidentals to reference the Moroccan sensibility of the architectural details

4. The kitchen cabinetry with wooden screen tracery on the upper cabinets, decorative lighting

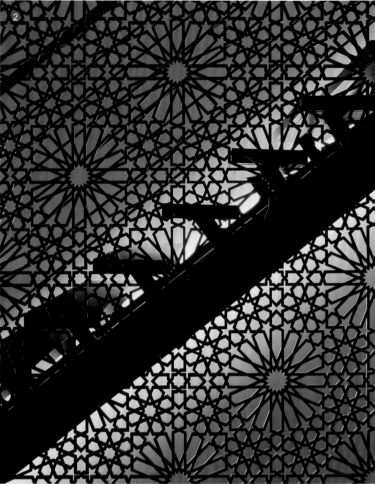

1. After taking the premises back to base building structure, a new open steel staircase became the chief unifying organising element for movement and visual focus. The floor lighting provides a clear path from the entry into the living area while highlighting the colour and texture of the wood-panelled walls

2. Most particularly the screen at the stair, which satisfies railing code requirements while adding a reach pattern that references traditional Moroccan tile mosaics but that are reinterpreted in a laser-cut metal screen with a bronze finish. The stair lighting is concealed at the stair stringer to create a glow that parallels the path of the treads and risers

3. The fireplace massing is original to the house, but the finishes were designed to completely transform this feature

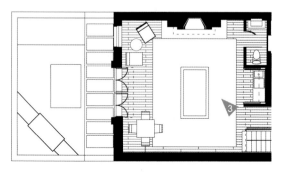

Billiards Room Plan

Master Bedroom+Dressing Room+Mater Bathroom Plan

1. While the house is largely detailed in a minimal and modernist manner, the client requested a house that also references the Moroccan aesthetic that he is especially fond of

2. Designers designed moments throughout the space that use both traditional and re-interpreted Moroccan motifs, including the custom stone mosaics at the fireplaces

3. The simple shape of wall and top reflects the characteristics of the overall space's detailed structure

4. The custom design includes special attention to lighting

10 Reconstruction of space

The reconstruction design of the home interior space refers to re-division of the space on the basis of original interior space and thus creates more convenient environment for people. It could give a comprehensive arrangement of the space's closure, anti-interference, privacy and people's requirements for the sight, sound, humidity and others.

In this case, the designers have introduced an integrated fixture that contains a kitchen, washing room and locker room into the interior space, and set it to the centre place, and given full consideration to the requirements of openness and privacy, function and streamline.

Project name: Loft Kullmann **Completion date:** 2010 **Location:** Hamburg, Germany **Designer:** GRAFT Gesellschaft von Architekten GmbH **Photographer:** GRAFT **Area:** 120 sqm

Master Plan

1. Kitchen
2. Bedroom
3. Washroom
4. Living space
5. Dining hall

Section Plan

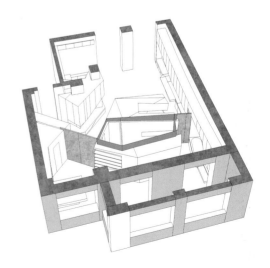

Panoramic Drawing

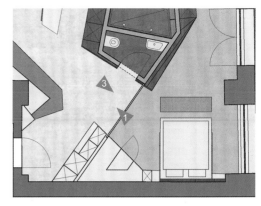

Washroom+Bedroom Plan

1. As with all renovations the existing building services and structure had to be incorporated in the overall design. This was achieved through the use of a free-standing walnut unit which functions as the heart of the apartment

2. This unit incorporates the kitchen, bathroom, and dresser, taking advantage of the proximity to the building services. Pieces are removed from the unit to allow natural light to penetrate deep within the loft

3. Flexibility in design was achieved through the use of ceiling-high, room-dividing sliding walls, allowing for multiple configurations of public and private space within the loft. The sliding walls, when retracted, are completely concealed within the service walls

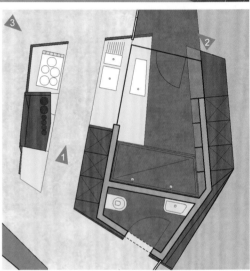

Kitchen+Washroom Plan

1. Materials like stone and wood bring warmth to the modern design

2. The centrepiece of the apartment is the wooden kitchen which is also half bathroom

3. Reportedly costing $200,000, the loft makes wonderful use of space with a freestanding centralised wood veneer kitchen

4. The space is thoughtfully designed to accommodate media and work needs as well as living and lounging needs

5. The place is a display of dramatic furniture and unexpected angles, a wonderful approach to contemporary design

6. The corner of washroom

7. Flanking the walnut core, are the service walls contrasted in white. These walls house the rest of the functional elements of the space

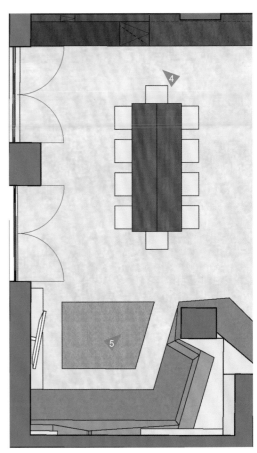

Living Space+Dining Hall Plan

11 The transition of space

The transition of the home space presents some definite fluidity. There may be varied constituent conditions with the different sizes, materials and shapes of the interfaces. There are also no defined spatial boundaries, as these enclosed interfaces are made up by elements such as the barrier top partition wall, screen and furniture at a bigger height.

In this case, the designer chooses the shelf as the separator between different interfaces, which divides the whole interior space into different areas including the entrance and the kitchen. The floating spatial effect makes the limited space more dynamic.

Project name: Apartament Formica **Completion date:** 2010 **Location:** Madrid, Spain **Designer:** Héctor Ruiz-Velázquez March **Photographer:** Pedro Martinez **Area:** 70 sqm

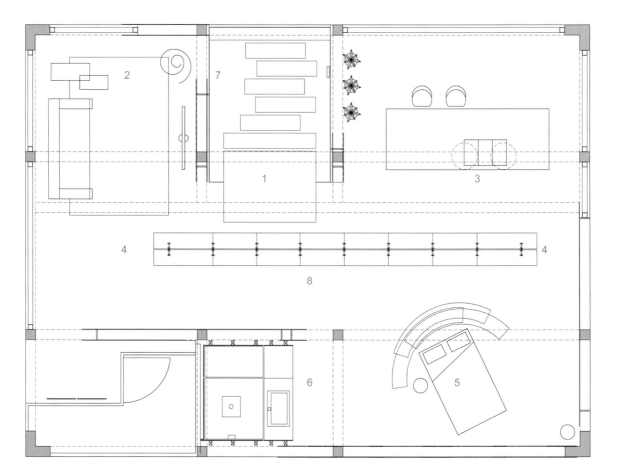

1. Entrance
2. Living room
3. Kitchen
4. Shelves
5. Bedroom
6. Bathroom
7. Closet
8. Corridor

Master Plan

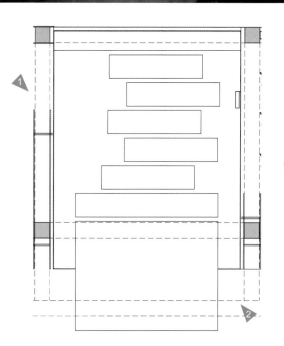

Entrance Plan

1. The vertical partition wall of the entrance hall also works as television background of the living room

2. The enclosing manner of the entrance space naturally separates this functional area from the whole space

3. The dividing form of the entrance foyer makes the layout of the space more natural and continuous

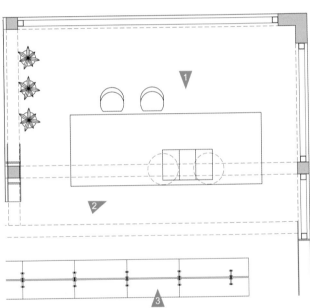

Kitchen Plan

1. As the heart of this spatial concept, the kitchen acts as the core to all other points in the house

2. The island, the epicentre of the space, is both a table and a bar, a place to grab a quick bite, or to share, to work alone or to gather around

3. The kitchen intertwines all the other spaces and functions of the home, unifying the other areas around it. It is also a living kitchen which grows in relation to the specific needs of the moment, without affecting the overall structure or shape. It grows in height with greater storage options, or in width for a greater workspace use, depending on the users' current livability needs. New esthetic features are added to the traditional kitchen to make this central space versatile. The goal is to unite food and culture, moving away from the typical concealment of kitchen items and developing a contrary concept, one of display. Through a network of shelves, the kitchen becomes a bookshelf, a partition, a pantry… taking on a sculpture-like visibility that begs to be seen

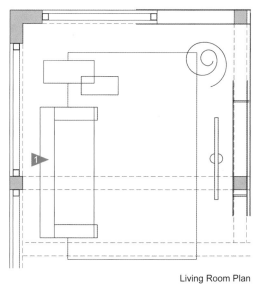

Living Room Plan

1. The simplicity of the unifying concept achieved in this space makes this project an innovative and unique example of modern architecture, a perfect combination

2. Its stone-like appearance used on horizontal planes of only 12mm is vividly contrasted with the bright yellow of the vertical surfaces, a combination of classic and modern, where the same material, the compact Top, takes on a completely different look because of how its use was carefully chosen

3. The fluid dividing manner makes the washroom more flexible

4. 80 square metres surrounding a nerve centre of activities and enjoyment for the home's residents.The shelf design allows you to put small kitchen items, such as spice racks, all the way up to large appliances anywhere. This means that the personality of the space depends entirely on personal taste. By placing the desired objects for all to see, completely different and personalised kitchens are created. The treatment given to this central space plays with fullness and emptiness, allowing light and air to play a leading role in the scene. It floats from a central volume, defying the laws of gravity and the concept of bases and structures, freeing the floor from all the bulk we are used to, that rather contaminates our spatial vision

12 The intention of space

The intentionality of the home space can be reflected by the virtuality and ambiguity of the space division which can be carried out in flexible ways that endow people's imagination and perception by the integration of the long, medium and close shots. In this way, the spatial form can enjoy abundant levels and strong fluidity. The approach of segmentation that forms the space image includes the railings, shelves, pergolas, the hollow partition walls, furniture, plants, water and lights.

In this case, the designer chooses the glass partition and the French sliding door as the main segmentation approaches of the linear space, while the introduction of the courtyard view makes the whole space more diversified.

Project name: 31 Blair Road **Completion date:** 2009 **Location:** Singapore City, Singapore **Designer:** Ong&Ong Pte Ltd **Photographer:** Tim Nolan **Area:** 306 sqm

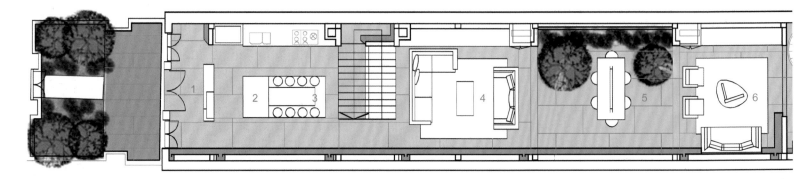

Master Plan

1. Entrance
2. Kitchen
3. Dining
4. Living room
5. Study room
6. Family room

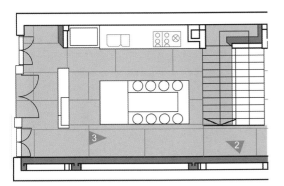

Entrance+Kitchen Plan

1. Moving past the thick bamboo garden in front, one then has an unobstructed, continuous view through the building, breathing space into this long, narrow terrace plot. This spaciousness is amplified by a fixed furniture wall that runs throughout the entire length and height of the house, unifying all activities within each level

2. Inspiration was taken from the smallest details on the existing façade, such as the bamboo motifs, which was subtly employed throughout the project

3. Each area is further defined by the use of subtle cove lighting and recesses in the walls, creating a variety of atmospheres

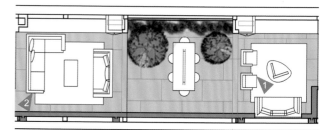

Living Room+Study Room+Family Room Plan

1. The choice of natural materials does not draw attention away from the design's historic aspects, but instead serves to compliment them

2. Monochromatic tones were used throughout to emphasise the project's alignment with conservation efforts of the site

1. The beauty of the house is its neutral environment

2. The inventive response was to raise the ceiling to make additional space in the roof, creating a mezzanine space on the second floor

3. To resolve lighting issues, a jack roof was built to allow large amounts of light in, which formed a bright and breezy space

13 To introduce new space

Sometimes, it is necessary to introduce new spaces into the creation of home space. This kind of approach redefines the original space by means of "Quadratic Definition" just as constructing a small room in a big space, by which the design can express its own wishful thinking while getting rid of all the original limits and constraints. The decorative approach is largely adopted in modern home design.

In this case, the designer introduces the style design of a streamline corridor into the original layout and then sets the bedrooms and the washing rooms on each side of the corridor and moreover there are directive round patterns on the floor of the corridor. The designer aims to create a vertical space with a sense of scale and depth while forming a melodic and canorous comparison.

Project name: Ruiz-Maasburg Penthouse **Completion date:** 2009 **Location:** Madrid, Spain **Designer:** Héctor Ruiz-Velázquez **Photographer:** Pedro Martínez **Area:** 60 sqm

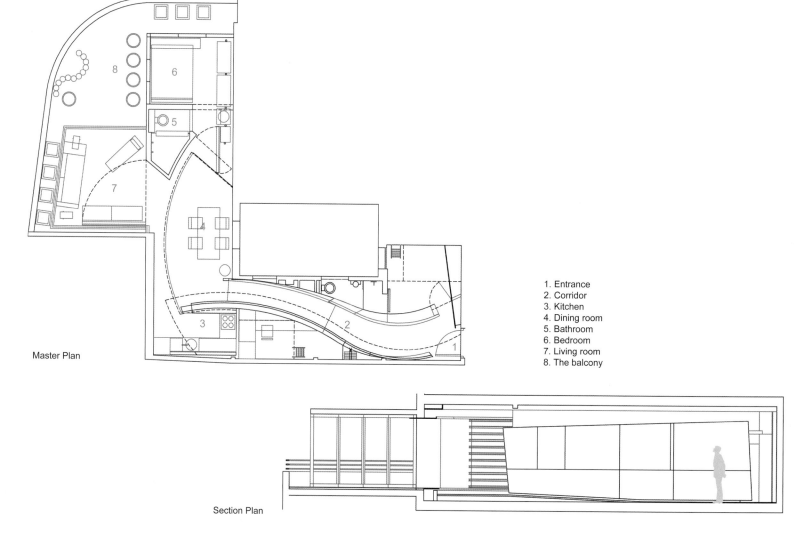

Master Plan

1. Entrance
2. Corridor
3. Kitchen
4. Dining room
5. Bathroom
6. Bedroom
7. Living room
8. The balcony

Section Plan

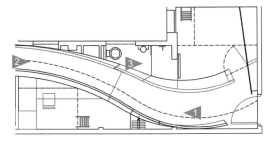

Entrance+Corridor Plan

1. A dynamic axis that emerges from the entrance leaves static spaces on both sides of the three-dimensional sinuous diagonal. Designer uses certain black points and surfaces in order to give scale and depth and thus create a complementary and melodic contrast

2. This hallway seems to defy gravity and logic and thus changes unexpectedly the perception of space according to the user and his movement through them. Thus it creates a completely fluent and dynamic space in a static surrounding

3. This tiny penthouse apartment in Madrid packs a punch - at just 60 square metres (about 650 square feet); the small space was designed to be super efficient and unique. It's especially interesting to see how architect made use of forced perspective and curves to make the space appear larger

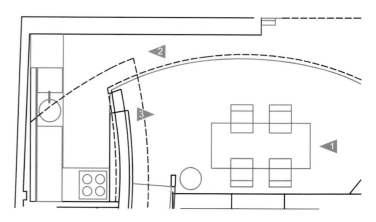

Dining+Kitchen Plan

1. Designer has transformed the attic space of an early 20th century building in Madrid, into a new living space with a variety of levels

2. The white colour and the lighting are further tools of design

3. The white colour and its multiple nuances of shadows created by light give a feeling of profundity and wideness

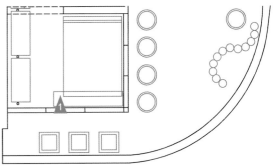

Bedroom Plan

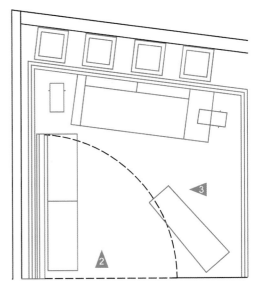

Living Room Plan

1. If fit in all the functions in an insufficient surrounding, the space would have collapsed, occupied by all useless things, and would thus have given view to the bare dimensions of the hardly hidden functions. In this way designer has used basic theatre tricks like forced perspectives in order to achieve much wider spacial perceptions

2. The far-from-standard shapes and curves mimic the homeowner's flow and use of space and the additional 50 square metres of adjacent terrace space was integrated into the home to further maximise the sightlines and openness

3. In this attic of only 60 square metres inside and 50 square metres of terrace/patio in the centre of Madrid, designer tried to use every centimetre of space available, combining efficiency, spirit and sensibility by means of aesthetics and function

14 The alternation of space

The combination of the home space can be showcased in interactively embedded ways, which can integrate the advantages and characteristics of different spaces as well as cover the shortages.

In this case, the designer implants a floor of bedroom space in the original open space with a strong linear sense and uses the space under the bedroom as the living room. The colour scheme of all the materials and the explicit directivity of the lines coordinate and unite the different functional areas and spatial environments. The introduction of the new space makes the open and spacious interior space more abundant.

Project name: Ceramic House **Completion date:** 2010 **Location:** Madrid, Spain **Designer:** Héctor Ruiz-Velázquez **Photographer:** Pedro Martinez **Area:** 54 sqm

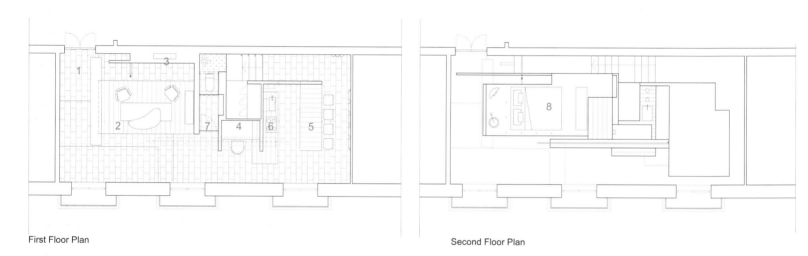

First Floor Plan

Second Floor Plan

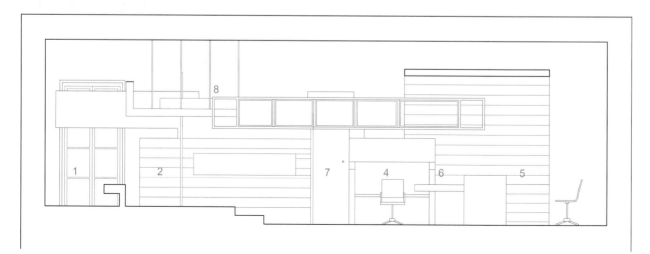

Section Plan

1. Entrance
2. Living
3. Fireplace
4. Office
5. Dining
6. Kitchen
7. Toilet
8. Bedroom

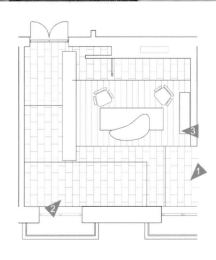

1. Where roominess, brightness and time flow in a multifunctional space without corners or precedence

2. The result is the power to move around in few square metres at different heights, going up and down, offering a new experience of roominess in the context of a home to explore the space

3. It is about expanding the parameters of interior design as well as the conventional trends of arrangement

Entrance+Living+Fireplace Plan

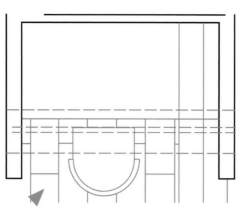

Office Plan

1. Every one of the rooms or points of the home can be located by specifying the axis of coordinates

2. The spatial flexibility that transforms this home is an innovative housing concept which adapts itself to the actual necessities and to the new usages

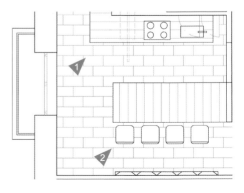

Dining+Kitchen Plan

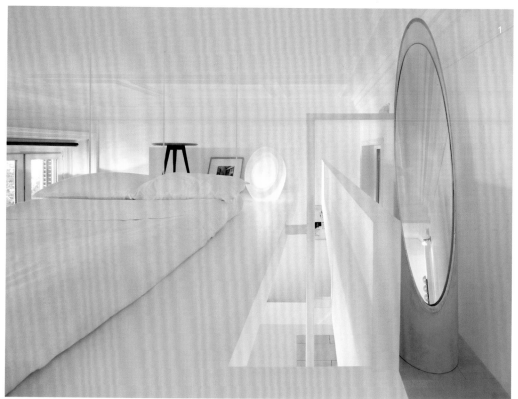

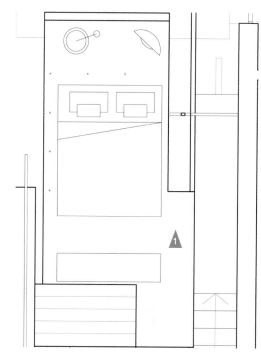

Bedroom Plan

1. The transition between the rooms is continuous and lets the movement flow freely across the numerous levels

2. The ceramic transforms itself into an excellent dynamic entity

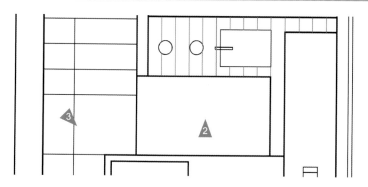

Toilet Plan

15 The layering of space

The dimension of the home space can be decided by the amalgamation and permeation between different enclosed interfaces or sometimes by men's visual association. The variation of the space dimension can make the plane layout more flexible while enhancing the sense of scale and depth of the space.

In this case, the most remarkable highlight goes to the courtyard design in the centre of the layout. The designer designs it as the central pivot of the circulation, a patio providing the interior space with natural lights as well as the visual focus. Moreover, the plants in the courtyard also increase the ecological significance of the interior space. The diversity of the plants and the transparency of the partition in the courtyard effectively intensify the sense of hierarchicy of the whole space.

Project name: 72 Sentosa Cove **Completion date:** 2009 **Location:** Sentosa Cove, Singapore **Designer:** Ong&Ong Pte Ltd **Photographer:** Ong&Ong Pte Ltd **Area:** 308 sqm

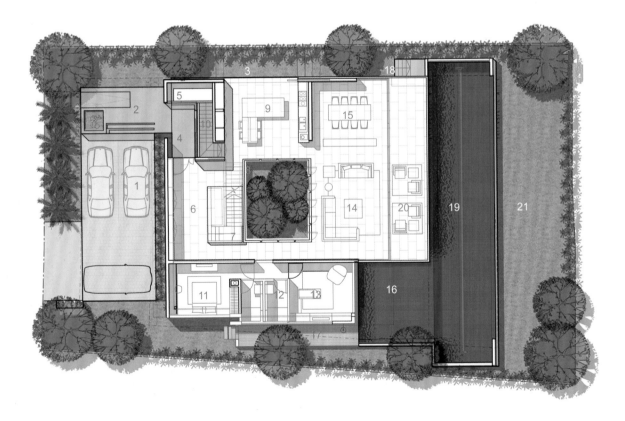

Master Plan

1. Covered carpark
2. Forecourt
3. Service access
4. Entrance
5. Storage
6. Foyer
7. Staircase
8. Garden
9. Kitchen
10. Service staircase
11. Guest bedroom
12. Powder room
13. Yoga room
14. Living
15. Dining
16. Jacuzzi
17. Outdoor shower
18. Outdoor staircase
19. 16-metre swimming pool
20. Outdoor deck
21. Garden

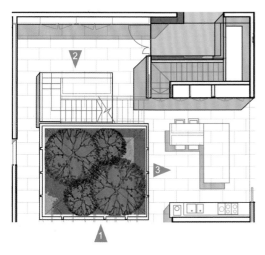

Foyer+Garden+Kitchen Plan

1. The internal spaces face inward into a multifunctional courtyard which acts as circulation pivot and light well, while also serving as a visual focal point. Dense foliage also provides a natural means for additional privacy

2. This is a home that can endure the tropics with minimal environmental impact, by tapping on available resources

3. The interweaving of the gardens and kitchen space has greatly blurred the boundaries of indoor and outdoor

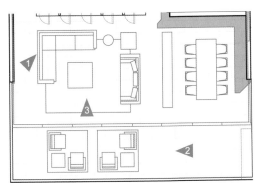

Living+Dining+Outdoor Deck Plan

1. Each level catering to various social and entertainment needs while also accommodating each family member's individual need for solitude

2. This is first and foremost a home for an active couple and their kids. For this, a lap pool ensures that their fitness needs are adequately taken care of

3. The house is conceived as a mass container that faces towards its interior, around a central courtyard that behaves as an inter-connector, and functions at the same time, as a circulation pivot, a light well, a ventilation exhaust and a visual landscape focal point

1. The client wished to maximise the buildable area of the house and at the same time achieve the most privacy possible for the design, taking into consideration that this plot is located between neighbouring houses

2. A pitched roof, with a series of repeating slopes, also generates additional skylight openings
3. The design of the house was figured as a building that adapts to the climatological conditions of the surroundings as well as to the specific natural resources available in the area (sun, light, wind, rain, topography) with the purpose of reducing the environmental impact of the traditional preconceived home

16 From interior to exterior

Among the combinations of the home space, the integrated combination is the most pervasive mode, which unites and harmonises the natural environment and the interior space by the transparent and flexible approaches to the mobile space. In this way, the scope of the design content of the home space turns broader in consideration of not only the relationship between the physical and virtual body of the interior space but the continuity between the interior and exterior space.

In this case, the open French window offers favourable condition for the connection of the interior and the exterior. The terrace, the swimming pool, the Greenland landscape and the interior environment echo each other, creating a flowing spatial ambience.

Project name: Waterpatio **Completion date:** 2008 **Location:** Odessa, Ukraine **Designer:** Drozdov & Partners Ltd. **Photographer:** Andrey Avdeenko **Area:** 725 sqm

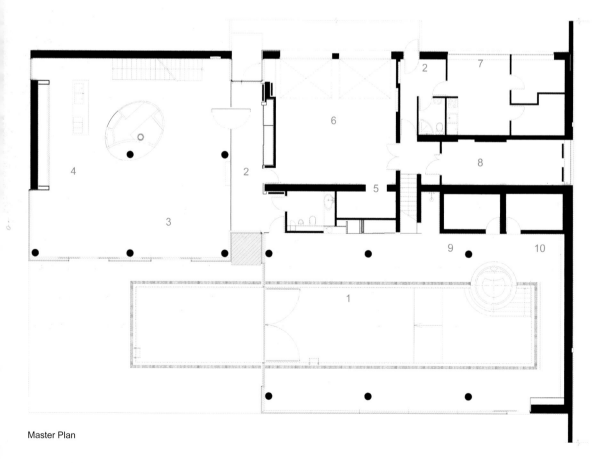

1. Swimming pool	6. Garage
2. Hall	7. Domestic
3. Living room	8. Technical room
4. Kitchen – dining	9. Sauna
5. Storage	10. Hamam

Master Plan

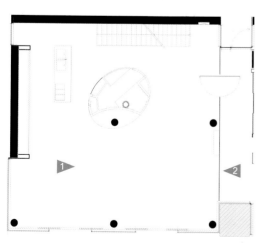

Living Room Plan

1. The entire space opens towards the sea. In addition to the outer sea horizon, which is a typical feature of any seaside house, designer introduced another water surface – that of the swimming pool, which enhances the visible proximity of the sea. The swimming pool is composed of two parts that can be separated or joined together depending on the season. Water element is the heart of the house, which explains its name: Waterpatio

2. The location of the house itself was largely determined by the desire to preserve as many of the existing trees as possible. Another important factor was the necessity to create a harmonious interrelation between the house, the garden and the sea view. These three environments are placed each along its own line and they interact in a variety of ways, depending on the position of the observer, whether it is the garden, the house or the mirador

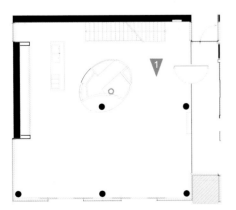

Living Room Plan

1. The central entrance into the house divides it into two functional blocks. The lower block contains a garage, a storage room, and the so called wellness zone, with a swimming pool, sauna and hamam. The other is the living block. The skylight in the hall makes this division even more distinctive. When entering the house one immediately understands the interrelation between different zones

2. The contrast between open and closed spaces continues in the way that how the house faces the street with its closed side and opens towards the sea and the garden

1/2. The flared space of the upper floor opens towards the sea horizon through the master bedroom and bathroom and shows a never-ending "marine" movie

17 Wandering space

In the home space, human actions and activities are limited by the established spatiality. Once the interior space is defined, it boasts some ability of restricting the life style, which may lead to a series of contradictions and problems. Men's employment of the interior space constitutes the main factor of the psychological changes. Therefore, the designers may consciously make use of the psychological characteristics of people to hammer out the relationship between the spatial condition and human actions so as to construct a suitable and favourable living environment.

In this case, the designer designs an elegant entrance space for a young couple. As a place to communicate with the other areas, the two-level-high entrance mass that is divided by the revolving door will lead the guests to wander between the swimming pool and the living room.

Project name: LA House **Completion date:** 2009 **Location:** Londrina, Brazil **Designer:** Studio Guilherme Torres **Photographer:** MCA Estúdio **Area:** 410 sqm

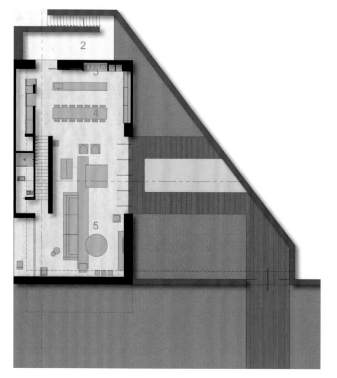

First Floor Plan

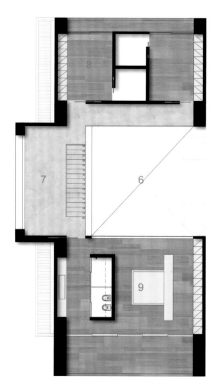

Second Floor Plan

1. Entrance
2. Lobby
3. Kitchen
4. Dining room
5. Living room
6. Overhead

7. Corridor
8. Dressing room
9. Master bedroom

Living Room Plan

1. The main concept of breaking paradigm takes place right at the entrance: the entrance gate leads the visitor to walk around the pool and into the house by double-height atrium, where the whole house communicates

2. The house, designed for a young couple, abolished traditional divisions and spaces. Downstairs, the living area acts as a liaison between the inside and outside through the large pivoting doors

3. The wall hides the volume of single staircase

4. Simple solutions and a few materials, but used in generous amounts confer personality and a timeless touch to this design, which shows a simple way of living

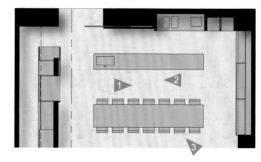

Kitchen+Dining Plan

1. The kitchen is integrated into the environment, with a niche where the stoves were installed, and even the charcoal grill
2. The dining area is perfectly integrated into the kitchen and living room, an ideal situation and true, eliminating the duplication of existing spaces as in current projects

Master Bedroom Plan

1. The master bedroom is separated from the living room by a glass wall, revealing to the cube of masonry houses toilets and showers

2. Sink and closet are integrated into the sleeping space

STRUCTURE DESIGN PRINCIPLES

18 Coordination of the plane

In home design, the plane layout plays an important role in forming the total design quality. As the essential factor of the space definition, the structure design of the ground can always be took into consideration as a whole element, which defines the scope of the used space with its smooth basal plane. Serving as the plane for people's activities and the display of furnishings, the ground has always been built as a secure and hard-wearing surface to make sure the adequate safety and sustainability.

In this case, the designer paves the ground with the floor board in the horizontal direction, which not only contributes to the interpenetration of the dining room, the living room and the kitchen, strengthening the fluidity, but echoes well with the wall space in colours.

Project name: Harlem Duplex **Completion date:** 2009 **Location:** New York, USA **Designer:** Studio SUMO **Photographer:** Studio SUMO **Area:** 158 sqm

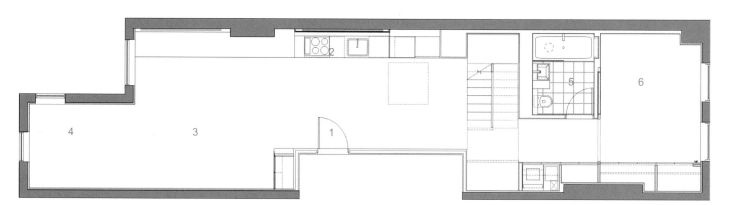

First Floor Plan

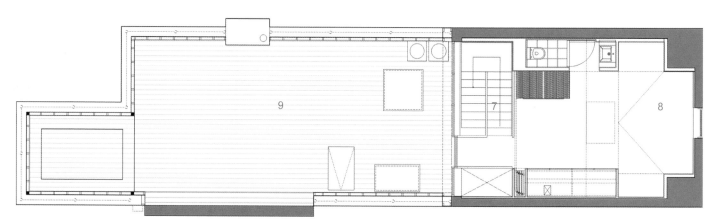

Second Floor Plan

1. Entrance
2. Kitchen
3. Living room
4. Dining room
5. Bath room
6. Dressing bar
7. Stair
8. Bedroom
9. Roof deck

1. The long and narrow horizontality was complimented by a vertical cut spanning the width of the apartment at its midpoint, and a new cantilevered steel stair and bridge was inserted. This light, harp-like structure coupled with a new bulkhead facade leading to a roof deck at the rear, brings light into the centre of the apartment

2. All the walls and ceiling surfaces of the HUD plan were removed and domestic programmes including kitchen, entertainment equipment, storage, and toilets were incorporated in linear strips along the party walls

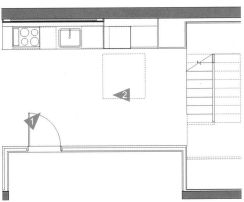

Entrance+Kitchen Plan

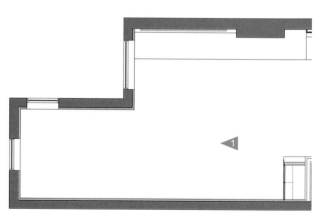

Living+Dining Plan

1. The approach to domestic programme created a linear openness with long views that are accentuated by new windows and skylights

2. The stair leads to the bedroom loft and the roof deck on either side of a steel bridge

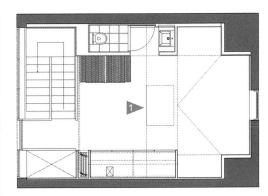

Bedroom Plan

1. The tall folded ceiling surface reveals the steep dormer of the building and is flanked by two consoles, one holding a toilet and sink, the other a closet. These consoles also hold a rack for the owner's sneaker collection

2. The wood deck with flush skylights is beyond, providing a horizon to the tall compact bed/shower loft. When privacy is required, the space can be also closed off with a series of pocketing door panels

3. A hi-gloss ceiling bounces light onto the consular glass ribbons which further illuminates the space

19 The basic point of division

There are many kinds of approaches of home space division: the girders and the pillars, as the fictitious definitive elements, are necessary elements of space division which cannot be ignored besides the application of immobile interfaces and furnishings. They constitute the three-dimensional virtual space on the rooftop and the ground in an axes array while being the constructional elements of the building. The size of space of them is closely bound up with the structural module, and therefore the girders and the pillars serve as the basic point of interior enclosure and division in the process of the home space design.

In this case, the designer retains the characteristics of the original building and makes a study on the colour, thus fusing them with the overall environment together artfully. Moreover, the ordering arrangement of the furnishings, combining the array of the girders and the pillars, further increase the four-dimensional attribute.

Project name: Island I **Completion date:** 2008 **Location:** Peloponnese Peninsula, Greece **Designer:** Cadena Design Group **Photographer:** Vangelis Paterakis **Area:** 340 sqm

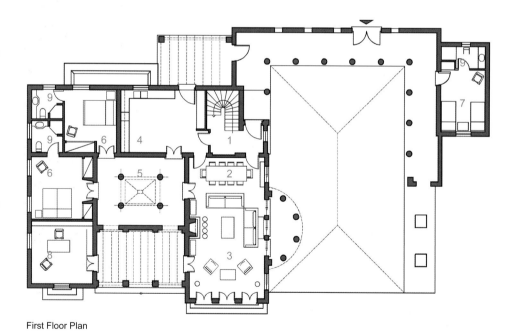

First Floor Plan

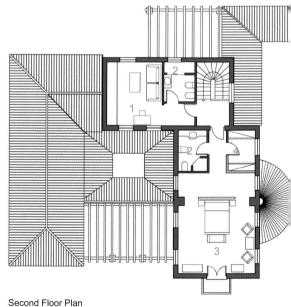

Second Floor Plan

1. Entrance
2. Dining
3. Living room
4. Kitchen
5. Patio
6. Bedroom
7. Guest room
8. Library/study room
9. Bathroom

1. TV room
2. Bathroom
3. Master bedroom
4. Wardrobe

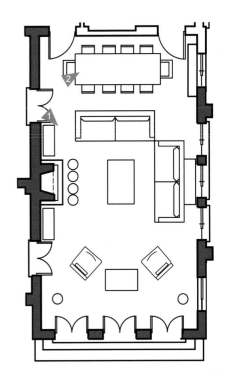

Living Room+Dining Plan

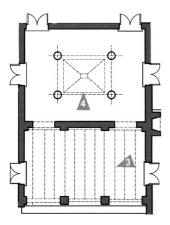

Patio Plan

1. Large windows ensure the flow of daylight to the dining room and living room. The comfortable sofas and armchairs enhance the cosy ambiance and the stateliness that impregnates the house

2. Paintings of contemporary Greek artists are displayed on the walls of the dining room. The light tones employed throughout the house confer charm and distinction to it

3. The patio is a space for enjoyment in the open air

4. The painted palms in the wall make up a place which invites us to dream

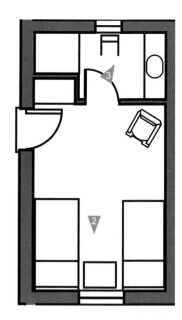

Guest Room Plan

1. The guest room is decorated in black and white which contributes to give a sober and elegant look

2. The arrangement of the stylish furniture was made in accordance with light providing liveliness to its rooms

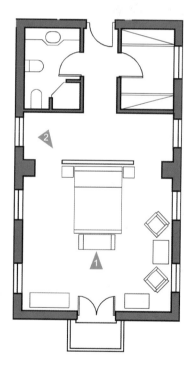

Master Bedroom Plan

1. The master bedroom is one of the most singular rooms of this house

2. The 4 windows create a delicate illuminated and friendly atmosphere and the balcony has a great view of Spetses Island

20 Surface decoration

During the process of the home space design, the wall, dividing the whole space on the ground into two totally different activity areas with its hypostatic plate, is the concrete definitive element of the interior space. The walls made from different materials are the main components of the enclosed interior space and support the whole architecture, providing the interior space with protection and privacy as the main decorative surface.

In this case, the designer designs the wall as a background that integrates different functional areas using simple modelling techniques and changes the main wall separating the living room from the gallery into a built-in bookcase in which the office space supplies such as the books and the facsimile apparatus are concealed. In this way, the office space is skillfully saved and the whole environment seems cleaner.

Project name: Apartment 3E **Completion date:** 2008 **Location:** Beijing, China **Designer:** Chien-Ho Hsu **Photographer:** Vector Architects **Area:** 265 sqm **Structure and material:** Corian, White Oak, Low-iron Glass

1. Foyer
2. Cleaning room
3. Wardrobe
4. Gallery
5. Dining room
6. Kitchen
7. Living room
8. Master bedroom
9. Master bathroom
10. Public bathroom
11. Storage
12. Guest bedroom
13. Children's room

Master Plan

1. The eleven-metre-deep living area provides a loft style space for relaxing, gathering and working, while the main wall between the living room and gallery has been transformed into a built-in bookcase while holds the books and fax machines as well as other work supplies

2. With the constraints of existing load-bearing wall structure, the reorganisation of spatial functions efficiently fulfills the basic needs for the family's daily life and creates a more flexible living space as well. The foyer leads to the gallery which naturally becomes a common space for the family before entering into the main living space and private rooms, and also provides a possible expansion for future needs

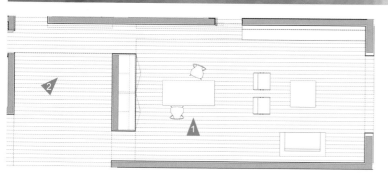

Gallary+Living Plan

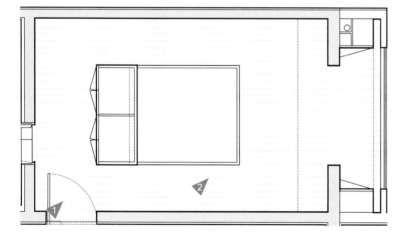

Bedroom Plan

1. A floating closet unit in the master bedroom not only provides a visual barrier from the living area, but also creates a buffer zone between the master bedroom and bathroom
2. The arrangement of the paintings and coffee table adds the simple space a sense of fun

2

1. All living functions are clearly defined, and yet the spaces retain a sense of continuity and cohesiveness

2. Open kitchen design encourages interactions between the kitchen and dining area, and the openness also improves the insufficient daylight from north-facing windows

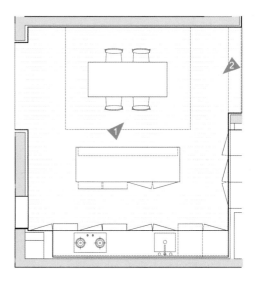

Dining+Kitchen Plan

21 The establishment of space's image

The roof shape in the home space design is the ultimate definitive element of the interior space structure. As the covering component of the interior space enclosure, it makes the architectural space the interior with its downward protective function. It plays an important role in visually shaping the image of the interior space.

In this case, the designer retained the historic concrete roof shape in order to reserve the characteristics of the original building while making a comparison with the modern life style. In the space configuration, the designer uses the brunet furniture and the hanging mirror to amalgamate the exposed concrete roof and the whole environment naturally.

Project name: Urbania **Completion date:** 2009 **Location:** Monterrey, México **Designer:** GLR Arquitectos / Gilberto L. Rodríguez **Photographer:** Jorge Taboada **Area:** 12,873 sqm **Awards:** Calli First Award, Category: Remodeling, XV Nuevo Leon Biennial of Architecture

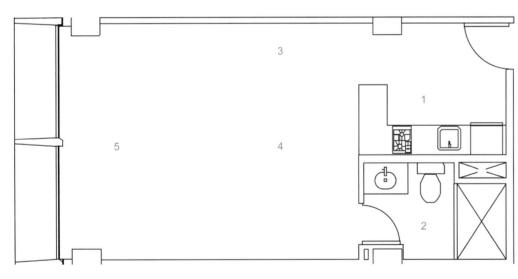

Master Plan

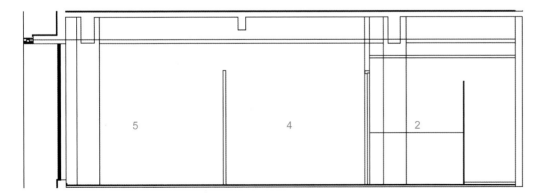

Section Plan

1. Kitchen
2. Bathroom
3. Dining room
4. Living room
5. Bedroom

1. The rest of the structure and original brick walls, were the subject of a careful restoration in order to rescue the architectural qualities of the building, which is an excellent example of modern architecture from the mid-twentieth century

2. The slogan used to promote these apartments is in itself a manifesto of a new way of life because it says "the city can only be lived in the city and this is the way it will be with Urbania"

3. In the interior was maintained, partly, the character of the building, leaving the ceilings with the original apparent 50 years old concrete

4. Without any doubt, the most important thing is that this work is a gamble for a new lifestyle that take advantage of what's already built and wants to regain the movement of a moribund area of Monterrey

22 The stillness of the space

Doors may define space and act as transitional elements for the interior home and they may become the intermediary of the interior and the exterior by breaking a continuous wall so as to connect different spaces together visually. As well as being the means of protection and directing traffic pathway, the function of the door changes with its location, size, style and structure. Sometimes, the style and type of the door define the overall style of the home space.

In this case, to meet the clients' demand of retaining the ambience of the traditional architecture while putting in some modern elements, the designer gives special attention to the style of the sliding door. Meanwhile, the large scale and proportion of the door can fill one with deep veneration, which implies the significance of the whole building.

Project name: Pacific Heights Townhouse Renovation **Completion date:** 2008 **Location:** San Francisco, CA, USA **Designer:** Feldman Architecture **Photographer:** Paul Dyer **Area:** 355 sqm

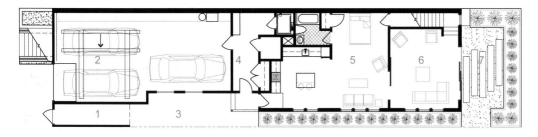

First Floor Plan

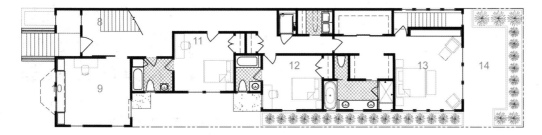

Secend Floor Plan

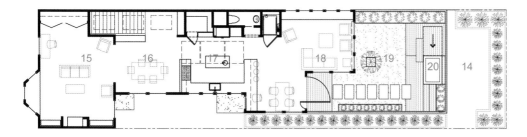

Third Floor Plan

1. Side entry
2. Garage
3. Side yard
4. Lobby
5. Guest suite
6. Living area
7. Rear yard
8. Entry
9. Playroom
10. Window seat
11. Bedroom 2
12. Bedroom 1
13. Master bedroom
14. Yard below
15. Living room
16. Dining room
17. Kitchen
18. Family room
19. Roof garden
20. Spa

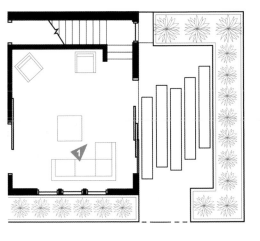

Living Area Plan

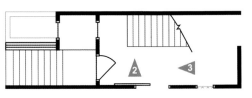

Entry Plan

1. The lower level living area with connection to garden. The owners wanted to maintain the building's traditional feel, but also to infuse some modern elements, so the house would be both more livable and reflective of their personalities

2. Open-riser stairs, a light well, and interior windows also allow light to filter down to the second floor hall

3. Sliding door flexibly separates the entrance and playroom

Third Floor Plan

1. The building is set off the south property line, which allowed the addition of numerous large windows along the length of the house

2. Most of the walls were removed from this floor to create spaces that are visually connected but functionally separated

3. Designer placed the living area on the top floor, where the light would be best and where, by removing a large portion of the rear space, a roof garden was created

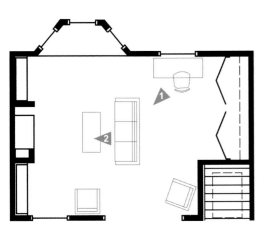

Living Room Plan

1. The Pierce Street Renovation involved updating and reconfiguring a 1906 stucco-clad Victorian architecture

23 The extension of the space

Windows, as the extension of the home space, not only play a significant role in forming the wall structure and layout of the whole space but also act as the important components of exterior style and characteristics of the building. The elements needed to be taken into consideration while configuring, selecting and designing the windows include the safety, the orientations, the daylighting, the quantity of rays required, the exterior landscape and the privacy.

In this case, the designer chooses the full-height French window in the living room to replace the fireplace and the door, which brings in the exterior view to the interior as much as possible apart from intensifying light in the interior.

Project name: Residence 1414 Renovation **Completion date:** 2008 **Location:** Austin, TX, USA **Designer:** Miro Rivera Architects **Photographer:** Paul Finkel, Piston Design **Area:** 5,658 sqm

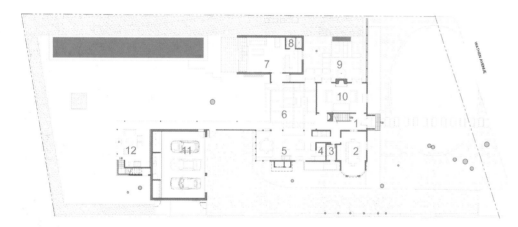

1. Entry
2. Dining
3. Powder bath
4. Pantry
5. Kitchen/breakfast
6. Family room
7. Den
8. Pool bath
9. Sideyard patio
10. Living room
11. Garage
12. Backyard patio

First Floor Plan

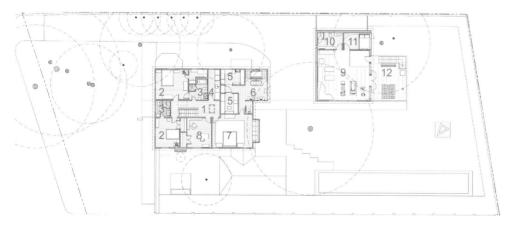

1. Hall
2. Bedroom
3. Bathroom
4. Laundry
5. Master closet
6. Master bathroom
7. Master bedroom
8. Office
9. Gym
10. Guest bathroom
11. Guest bedroom
12. Gym dock

Second Floor Plan

1. A large three-panel sliding glass door transformed the Den into an extension of the pool terrace. Pennsylvania bluestone is used extensively as the exterior paving material at the patios

2. Ipe wood is used extensively on the interior and the exterior of the house, including the wood band that wraps the Den, the countertop at the Den bar

3. Painted white gypsum board walls are combined with several carefully selected materials used repeatedly throughout the house to achieve a clean and balanced space that is not distracting

4. Stainless steel is the primary metal finished on the interior of the house. It can be seen in most of the appliances, at the shelves and open drawers in the kitchen & pantry. For stone finishes soapstone and carrera marble were selected. Soapstone comprises the kitchen countertops. Besides, the operable windows opened up the kitchen to the backyard

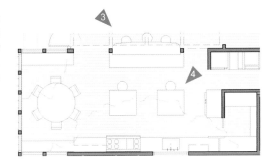

Dining+Kitchen Plan

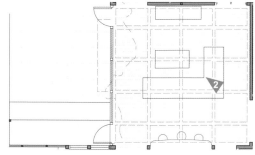

Living Room Plan

1. The material palette for the exterior of the house is simple as well. White painted wood lap siding is the main material on the exterior of the house. Any exposed metal structure is painted to match, while the two sidewalls at the entry to the house

2. Floor-to-ceiling windows replaced a fireplace and French doors in the rear-facing family room

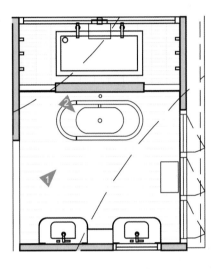

Master Bathroom Plan

1. Upon first impression the original house felt very confined and dark inside, so an important factor in the re-design was to open up the house to let in more light

2. Windows could introduce the outdoor environment into the inside

3. It was important to maintain a balance between the traditional aspects of the original house design and the modern updates that the clients desired, as well as provide a clean backdrop for the clients' extensive art collection. This was accomplished through choosing a simple material palette and by uncluttering the spaces within the house

24 The organisation of the vertical space

In the structural design of the home space, the staircase styling belongs to the domain of the vertical transportation system. In addition to performing the basic transport functions, the variation of the staircase styling has always been regarded as the principal part of the interior space design. Due to the bigger and bigger scale of modern home space, the new method of vertical migration has been added to the traditional horizontal migration. As a result, the original observing method of watching - from the bottom to the top - has gradually changed. The view point that had been neglected has been attached more importance because of the introduction of the interior stairs.

In this case, the designer's design of the staircase styling and the originality of the skin texture derive from the observation and comprehension the nature water. The clipper-built structure and the hole design on the surface make people experience the varied effects of light and shadow at different locations when shuttling back and forth on the stairs.

Project name: Uptown Penthouse **Completion date:** 2007 **Location:** Minneapolis USA **Designer:** ALTUS Architecture + Design **Photographer:** Dana Wheelock & ALTUS Architecture + Design **Area:** 250 sqm

Imagery: With the project's proximity to the Minneapolis Chain of Lake, the concept began with the metaphor of water

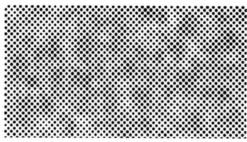

Manipulation: The image was pixelised to create a half-tone pattern reflecting the original water image. The pixelisation yielded cirecular references consisting of three diameters (3.5", 3" & 2.5")

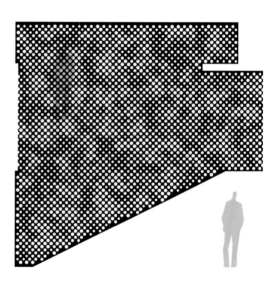

Resultant: The pixelated pattern was then overlayed on the flattened stainless steel panel layout shown above. The digital image was then used to instruct the computer guided laser cutting of the stainless steel panels

Master Plan

1. Entry
2. Kitchen
3. Living room
4. Dining room
5. Master bath
6. Master dressing
7. Master bedroom
8. Terrace
9. Laundry
10. Office/guest room
11. Dressing room
12. Bathroom
13. Power room

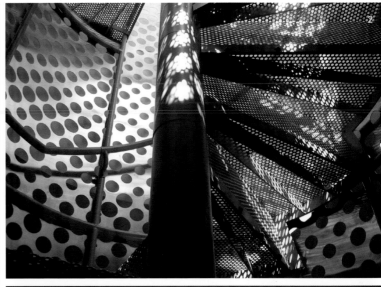

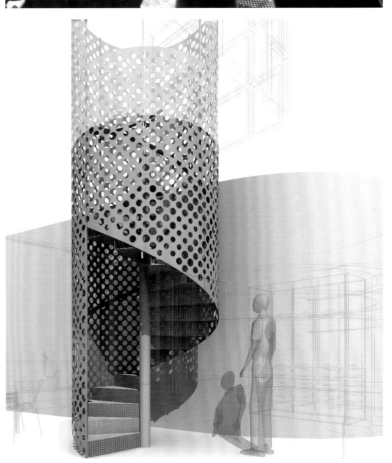

1. The concept for the stair began with the metaphor of water as a connection to the chain of city lakes. An image of water was abstracted into a series of pixels that were translated into a series of varying perforations, creating a dynamic pattern cut out of curved stainless steel panels. The result creates a sensory exciting path of movement and light, allowing the user to move up and down through dramatic shadow patterns that change with the position of the sun, transforming the light within the space

2. Detail interior view of spiral stair

3. Detail view of spiral stair screen

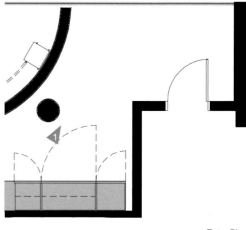

Entry Plan

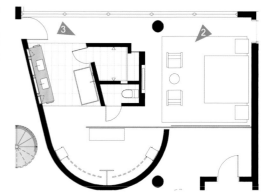

Master Dressing+Master Bedroom Plan

1. Upon entry, a curved wall of white marble dust plaster pulls one into the space and delineates the boundary of the private master suite

2. The master bedroom space is screened from the entry by a translucent glass wall layered with a perforated veil creating optical dynamics and movement. This functions to privatise the master suite, while still allowing light to be filtered through the space to the entry

3. Within the master suite a freestanding Burlington stone bathroom mass creates solidity and privacy while separating the bedroom area from the bath and dressing spaces. The curved wall creates a walk-in dressing space as a fine boutique within the suite. The suspended screen acts as art within the master bedroom while filtering the light from the full height windows which open to the city beyond

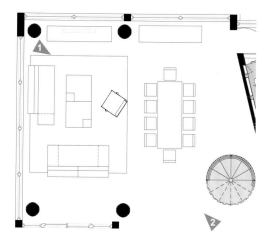

Living Room+Dining Room Plan

1. A custom perforated stainless steel shroud surrounds a spiral stair that leads to a roof deck and garden space above, creating a daylit lantern within the centre of the space

2. Designed for a young professional, the space is shaped by distinguishing the private and public realms through sculptural spatial gestures

3. The kitchen is composed of cherry and translucent glass cabinets with stainless steel shelves and countertops creating a progressive, modern backdrop to the interior edge of the living space. Suspended cabinet elements of Australian walnut float opposite the curved white wall and walnut floors lead one into the living room and kitchen spaces

4. The powder room draws light through translucent glass, nestled behind the kitchen. Lines of light within, and suspended from the ceiling extend through the space toward the glass perimeter, defining a graphic counterpoint to the natural light from the perimeter full height glass

25 Protection and decoration

The aesthetic attribute of the handrail is also crucial in the home design apart from its basic protective functions. It needs to maintain a coordinated and unified relationship with the whole interior style in terms of styling variation, colour scheme and texture contrast.

In this case, the designer makes the patio run through the four-storey space and moreover hopes to create an elegant space which can draw in the exterior view. Designed simply, the handrails are arranged in the linear array, which constitutes a perfect combination with the stairs and the patio while adding a vacant dynamic to the patio space. As the design of the handrail doesn't lead to any block of the environment, the lights penetrated the glass wall spray sufficiently on all the enclosed surfaces.

Project name: Narrow House **Completion date:** 2010 **Location:** Barcelona, Spain **Designer:** Jordi Antonijoan Roset, Francesc Solé Durany **Area:** 100 sqm

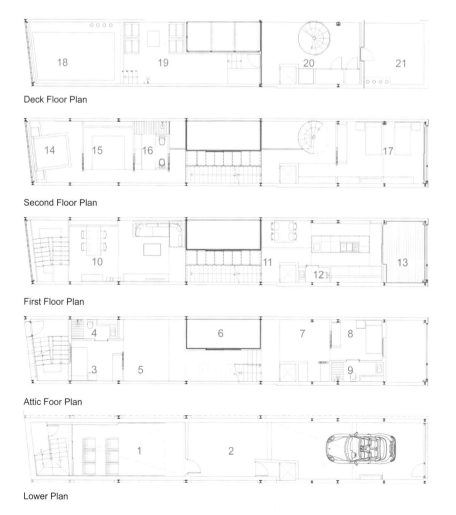

Deck Floor Plan

Second Floor Plan

First Floor Plan

Attic Foor Plan

Lower Plan

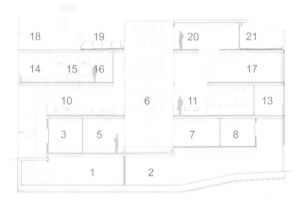

Section Plan

1. Cinema
2. Garage
3. Bedroom
4. Bathroom
5. Study hall/games
6. Patio/garden
7. Study hall/games
8. Bedroom
9. Bathroom
10. Living/dining
11. Kitchen
12. Toilet
13. Gallery
14. Bedroom
15. Dress room
16. Bathroom
17. Bedroom
18. Pool
19. Terrace
20. Laundry
21. Terrace

1. Designer wanted to create a dwelling space that was able to take advantage of the outdoors while avoiding the stress of the city

2. The form of the stair railing makes the vertical space be more light and simple

3. Materials such as wood, stone, warm paint colours, wallpaper and low ceilings convert the rooms to become comfortable warm living spaces

4. The setting of the rail does not affect the transparence of the overall space, but adds a rhythm for the horizinal space

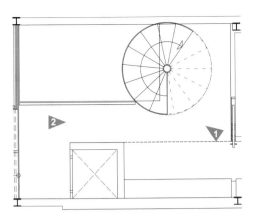

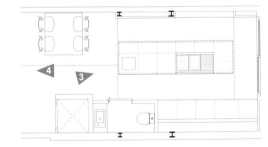

1/2. The ideas of the house are very well explained in section and are also reflected in the treatment of materials, which play a very important role

3. The kitchen that's connected with a gallery which can be converted as a terrace during the summer

4. Different rooms are built with large open spaces and communicate amongst themselves in an almost transparent way

Kitchen Plan

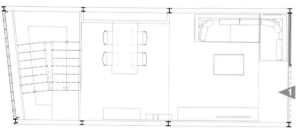

Living+Dining Plan

1. The guardrail has become the transparent enclosure interface of the living room, so as to enhace the fluid visual effect of the overall space
2. The client's requirements were basically the programme needs and the need of daylight. The plot is very narrow and they were worried about it. Catching the light became the most important aspect of the project

26 The re-creation of the interior space

The definite division of the home space can only be realised by the full-height partition walls, which can create the introverted spatial quality with a strong sense of closure.

In this case, the designer divides the open interior space into three parts in an orderly way by breaking the routine to integrate the partition wall and the cabinet. Standing over against the kitchen, one can feast his eyes on the natural landscape outside. The design of the full-height partition walls makes no difference to the spatial fluidity.

Project name: SODAE House **Completion date:** 2009 **Location:** Amstelveen, The Netherlands **Designer:** Cristina Ascensão (VMX Architects) **Photographer:** Jeroen Musch **Area:** 500 sqm **Awarded:** Nominated for the Amsterdam Architecture Prize 2010

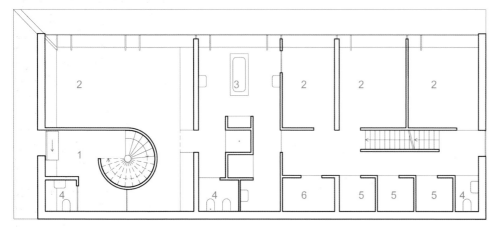

First Floor Plan

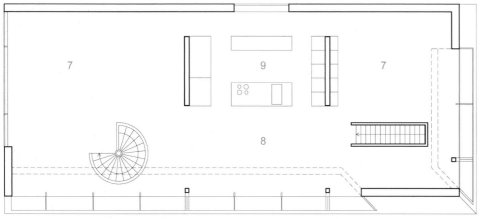

Second Floor Plan

1. Entrance
2. Bedroom
3. Bathroom
4. Toilet
5. Wardrobe
6. Laundry room
7. Living Space
8. Dining space
9. Kitchen

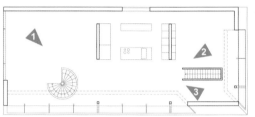

Living Space Plan

1. The deceptively simple form is the product of a creative interpretation of the restrictions imposed by the zoning plan

2. The obligatory chamfering of the volume was intended to result in a traditional Dutch gabled roof. Instead, designer turned this municipal stipulation into a tool for invention. The four sides of the basic volume are sliced in such a way that no two sides are the same. The end result of this subtle strategy is a highly distinctive form, an asymmetrical decahedron

3. Cutting right through this horizontal arrangement is a vertical separation between the parents' and the children's parts of the house. Each zone has its own entrance, stairs and bathroom in a clever interweaving of separate and shared use

1. The living room and kitchen are arranged in a loft-like space on the second floor

2. Inside the volume, each of the three floors has a different aspect. The living areas (eating, playing and working) are on the top floor which has the finest view

3. The sleeping area looks in the opposite direction where privacy is assured

4. The more intimate areas (bedrooms and bathrooms) are situated on the first floor, orientated towards the garden on the backside

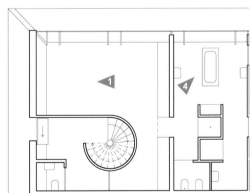

Bedroom Plan

27 Challenge limitation

There are many approaches to the established building structures in comprehensive home space design: it is workable to comply with the arrangement of the whole structure by making them in a visual order; it is also possible to make them live harmony with the whole space by exposing or discovering the building structures in the outstretched methods. The exposed structure, as a component of the whole architecture, stands for the style and the history of the building. In many modern interior design works, the designers choose to retain the original building components rather than disguising them aimlessly. In terms of the home interior design, however, there's more embodiment of individuality than the arrangement of decoration and display, while it is difficult to make any breakthrough in the spatial style. There's less and less structural restrict of this kind since the emergence of the newly developed materials in large scale. The leading style of the interior space composed by materials and structures rather than the additional ornamentation has become the new trend of the home space design.

In this case, the designer starts with design of frame construction of the building so that much design that conflicts with the interior design style is avoid. For instance, the large scale sliding door in the living room makes the space more spacious.

Project name: Chalon Residence **Completion date:** 2009 **Location:** Los Angeles, USA **Designer:** Belzberg Architects **Photographer:** Art Gray Photography **Area:** 725 sqm

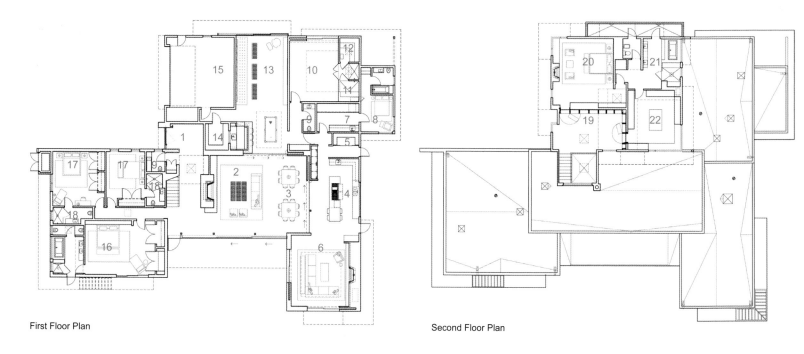

First Floor Plan

Second Floor Plan

1. Entry	7. Laundry	13. Theatre	19. Library
2. Living room	8. Maid's quarters	14. Wine cellar	20. Master bedroom
3. Dining room	9. Powder room	15. Garage	21. Master bathroom
4. Kitchen	10. Gym	16. Guest suite	22. Master closet
5. Pantry	11. Sauna	17. Bedroom	
6. Family room	12. Steam room	18. Bathroom	

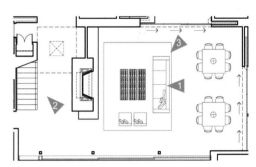

Living Room Plan

1. Belzberg Architects was brought in to design the house during the framing stage. The design strategy became more about coping with limitation and creating a narrative of space from what was previously defined and unsuccessful. In many respects, Chalon became about solutions rather than statements. The living room benefitted greatly from this bolder intervention by incorporating larger sliding doors

3. The previous incarnation of the structure failed to properly respond to both site and solar considerations. From these moments, a heavy emphasis was placed on opening the space up and out by pocketing doors and recapturing lost views. The layout originally relied on Feng Shui as the primary strategy for circulation and placement and was one which was continued in the final overall scheme

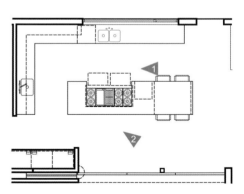

Kitchen+Dining Plan

1. In all forms, texture became the predominant answer and this theme was carried out at all scales

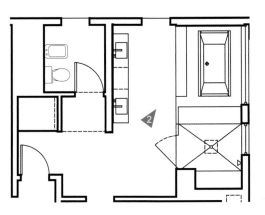

Master Bathroom Plan

1. The design strategy also directly informed the direction of how conditions were detailed and focus of how materials were treated as finishes

2. Texture became a device that functioned not only as a procedure of layering but as the end result; in other words, texture became both the means and the end

INTERFACE DESIGN PRINCIPLES

28 The tension of the vision

As people used to observe from the bottom to the top, the floor may be observed more frequently than the other interfaces. Meanwhile, the scale and the shape of the floor also imply the scope and function of the space. In a sense, the floor conveys the fictitious spatial information to people just like a grid and offers different visual experience.

In this case, the designer devises the random patterns with the limestone, unifying the open public area through dynamic colour changes. Moreover, the shape and size comparison of the stone work in concert with the decorative material on the wall, a kind of allusive relationship expressing a visual stretching force.

Project name: The Quogue House **Completion date:** 2010 **Location:** Dune Road, Quogue, New York **Designer:** Andi Pepper Interior Design **Photographer:** RAZUMMEDI **Area:** 738 sqm

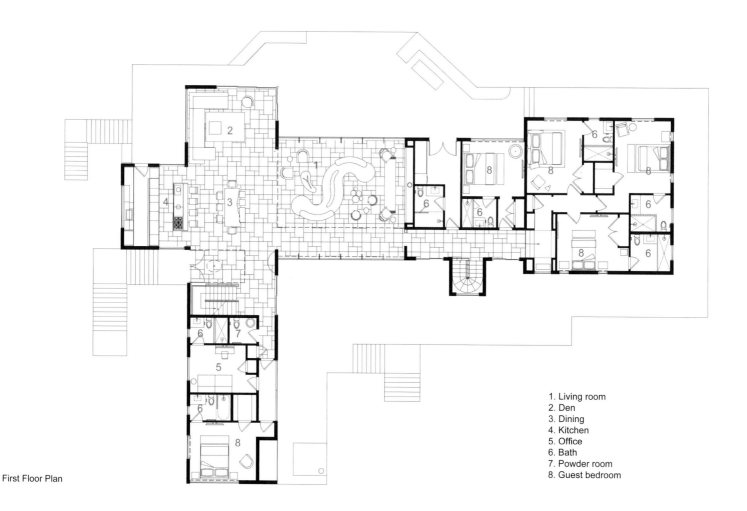

First Floor Plan

1. Living room
2. Den
3. Dining
4. Kitchen
5. Office
6. Bath
7. Powder room
8. Guest bedroom

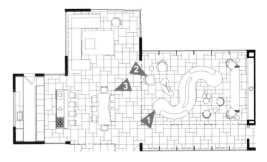

Living Room+Kitchen+Dining Plan

1. The living room was also gutted to allow for two-storey glass facades on both the north and south walls. This afforded an open plan allowing dramatic views of both the ocean and bay from the entrance. The large glass expanse becomes a huge window as well from the upper poolside terrace looking to the Atlantic

2. The living room features limestone flooring, a gas fireplace with leather walls and a dramatic bridge across the two-storey space to the master bedroom

3. An extension of the living room includes the dining area, kitchen and seating area, perched under an overhang

1. The second floor which overlooks the living room was gutted to accommodate a bar and lounge area looking down on the living room and through to the south water views. The flooring is wenge and the bar features a yellow light panel

2. Pictured here is the second floor seating area with views to the beach and ocean

1. Master bedroom with wenge flooring, a sculpted wood bed and lacquered cabinets provides both an intimate space and magnificent ocean panorama

2. The master bath with views to the ocean includes a marble sink countertop affixed to a glass wall with a light wall to the right

29 Flooring design and functional division

In home interior design, the different scales, proportions, and material qualities of the floor pavement imply the diversity and abundance of the spatial functions. Sometimes, the designers use different collage materials to produce distinct transition effect, while the same material is chosen sometimes to demonstrate the effect of contrast and conformity through the variation of the scale and ways of paving.

In this case, the designer chooses wood as the material of the floor pavement to create a comfortable and quiet space ambience, adopting the approach of differentiating the first floor and the second floor rather than making the partial changes. On the first floor, the pavement in vertical moulding combines all the public areas in an arranged order while implying the directivity of the spatial mobility; the pavement in diagonal lines on the second floor conveys the flexibility and dynamic of the private space.

Project name: Zhong Neng Real Estate- Evian Stacked Villa **Completion date:** 2007 **Location:** Chengdu, China **Designer:** Fanghuang, Hong Kong **Photographer:** Wang Jianlin **Area:** 155 sq

The establishment of the style means the recognition of the culture. The floral patterns sofas, simple and elegant walls, the leisure balcony with fragrance of the soil and the silent fireplace create a quiet and cosy atmosphere that gets rid of the bustling citylife. Here, what you'll get will be only the green oasis. The designer aims to employ the beige and white colour to build a warm and pastoralism house

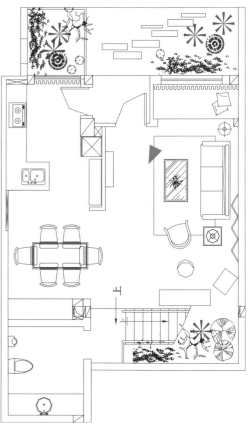

First Floor Plan

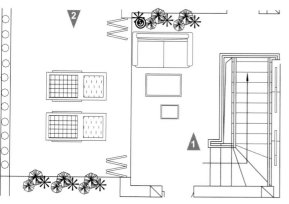

Second Floor Plan

1. The arrangement of the terrace helps the owner enjoying leisure time everyday
2. Town of Evian - terrace rest area

30 Route design

In home space design, the changes of texture cannot be ignored apart from the quality and scale that need to be taken into account when choosing the material of the floor pavement. This kind of change can not only provide plentiful visual enjoyment but form a strong sense of order and imply the directivity of the space, which is visually effective in changing the size of the space and the human action and psychology.

In this case, the designer chooses French white marble as the material of pavement of the public area. The stone texture with clear vertical lines increases the feeling of depth of the space while implying the walking direction as well.

Project name: No.12 Villa **Completion date:** 2010 **Location:** Shanghai, China **Designer:** Zhao Muhuan /Mohen Design International **Photographer:** Zhou Yuxian **Area:** 330 sqm **Main materials:** Cherry wood finishes, French white marble, oxidation Magnesium plate, stainless steel plated black titanium, iron board grilled white paint, mosaic parquet, cork flooring, matt cherry flooring

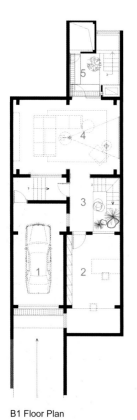

B1 Floor Plan

First Floor Plan

Second Floor Plan

Third Floor Plan

1. Garage
2. Study
3. Corridor
4. Media
5. Garden
6. Living room
7. Dining room
8. Kitchen
9. Dressing room
10. Bedroom
11. Leisure area
12. Master bedroom
13. Master bathroom

1. The horizontal texture of the floor is perpendicular to the visual line, which together with the top enhances the sense of layer

2. The straight line of the floor pavement suggests the direction of walking

3. The setting of the ground landscape and fixtures has created a perfect environment for people to stop and appreciate

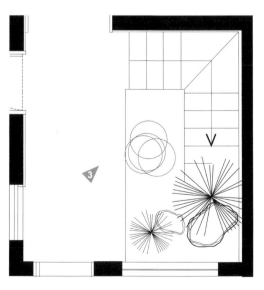

Corridor Plan

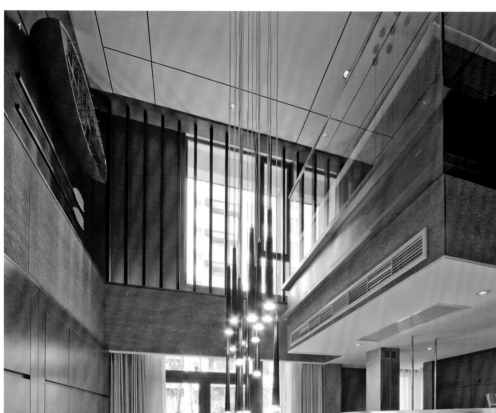

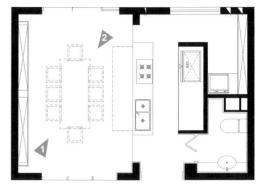

Kitchen+Dining Plan

1. The linear floor texture integrates with the composition style of the overall space

2. The floor texture has enhanced the sense of depth and movement

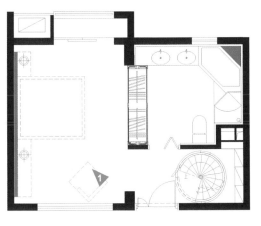

Master Bedroom Plan

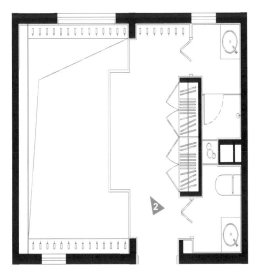

Dressing Room Plan

1. The specular reflection together with the metal accessories makes the overall atmosphere be more light

2. The uncontinuous lines of the floor generate a wave-like visual effect and subtly associate with the distant ship devices; the hanging lights with vertical lines become the visual focus of the space

31 The transition of the areas

In home space design, the variation and transition of the floor depend on the changes of the spatial function. Different spatial functions have their own area coverage. The connection of these areas can be realised by changing the method of the floor pavement, the floor colour, the material, the scale and proportion as well as the height.

In this case, the designer employs the visual contrast to achieve the transition and change of the floor by subsiding the dining room and the kitchen, which forms a new spatial sequence through the changes of the viewpoint during the process of walking.

Project name: Parksite **Completion date:** 2009 **Location:** Rotterdam, The Netherlands **Designer:** Doepel Strijkers Architects in collaboration with LEX-Architecten BNA **Photographer:** Maarten Laupman **Area:** 260 sqm

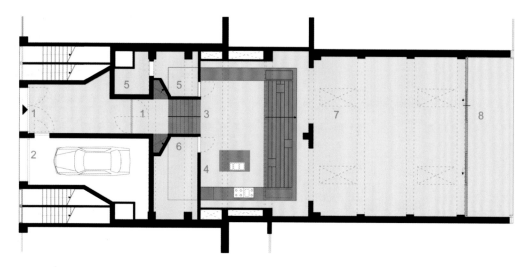

Firsr Floor Plan

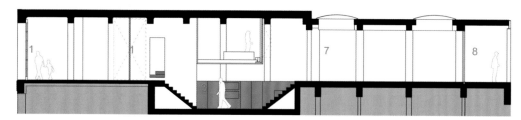

Section Plan

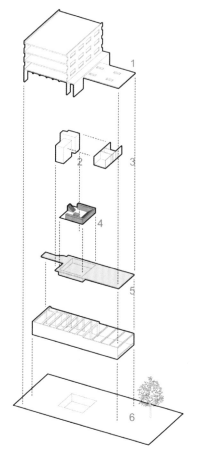

Axonometric Drawing

1. Entrance hall
2. Garage
3. Dug out
4. Kitchen
5. Storage
6. Scullery
7. Living room
8. Terrace

Entrance Hall Plan

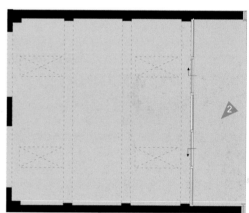

Living Room Plan

1. The existing garage is treated as a shell with a new concrete floor with integrated services. This floor flows through the house connecting the large entrance hall on the street side

2. This former ambulance garage in the centre of Rotterdam borders on a secluded park. Replacing the rear wall with a large glass window creates a direct relationship to it

3. The flexibility of the large over dimensioned living room and multitude of different atmospheres in the house make it a liveable space that is being fully exploited by its new inhabitants in a playful manner

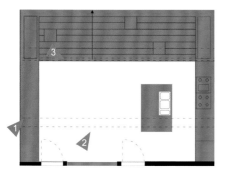

Kitchen+Dining Plan

1. As one moves under the box, views of the park emerge, creating a sequential build up of spaces culminating in the breathtaking view of this green oasis

2. Loose blocks on the staircase form informal chairs or function as tables depending on the situation. The suspended light box functions as a focal point in the movement from the front of the house to the garden

3. Custom-made cupboard, kitchen and stairs finished in bright orange polyurethane, link the dugout to the entrance hall on the street side and the living room on the park side

1. Although the intervention seems simple, a number of challenges presented themselves in practice. The entire dugout and suspended light box stand completely free from the existing structure. Nine 20-metre-deep piles prevent the dugout from floating due to the pressure from the ground water. The weight of the light box is transferred through consoles to the concrete construction of the dugout. In order to comply with building regulations an intricate mechanical ventilation system has been implemented in combination with floor heating

2. The dugout in the middle of the building generates height for a second level. A polycarbonate lightbox with integrated LED lights houses the bedrooms and spans the space above the living-kitchen

32 The tactile experience of walking

In home space design, the change of the floor material plays a key role in bringing about the tactile experience besides conveying the visual richness. The immediacy of men's feeling when walking makes the changes of the floor material - whether it is thick or thin, concave or convex, cold or hot, a direct reaction in men's sense organs and helps them make judgement about the spatial ambience. So to speak, the changes of the floor texture bear a direct influence on people's space judgement.

In this case, the designer chooses the wood floor as the paving material. The natural timber texture presents distinct undulate changes, on which one can experience the comfort and cosiness of the space. Meanwhile, the arrangement of the artworks enhances the spatial effects.

Project name: Penthouse Downtown Montreal **Completion date:** 2010 **Location:** Montreal, Canada **Designer:** Rene Desjardins **Photographer:** André Doyon **Area:** 307 sqm

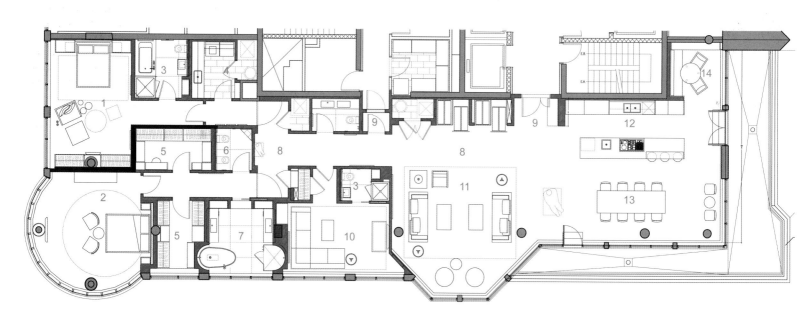

Master Plan

1. Children bedroom	8. Hall
2. Master bedroom	9. Entrance
3. Bathroom	10. Little living room
4. Washroom	11. Living room
5. Walk-in closet	12. Kitchen
6. Study	13. Dining room
7. Master bathroom	14. Small dining room

1. The apartment comprises two zones: on one side, the shared areas: the living room, dining room and kitchen as well as a living area/home theatre; and on the other, the private quarters of the client and his son. Detailed work began on the interior envelope, playing with different coatings and colours for the volumes, using whites and shades of grey and brown to create a pared-down, warm environment

2. Each recessed lighting fixture has two spots, multiplying the lighting possibilities with a minimum of means

3. Window treatments received particular attention. Sheets of fabric combining natural fibres with threads of stainless steel-completely invisible when raised-descend from the ceiling at the touch of a button to temper the light and preserve privacy. In order to maintain the spirit of a loft, the structural columns were simply sanded down and painted in the same shades and finishes as the walls

Living Room Plan

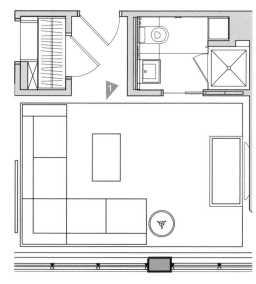

Little Living Room Plan

1. The designer suggested a space much like the large contemporary lofts of Manhattan or Los Angeles, a loft that would speak of calm and comfort yet look out over the continually changing showcase of the city. The living area/home theatre adjoining the living room carries over the same natural shades. The wolf on the wall (by Josée Pedneault) provides an unusual and humourous note that sets the tone for this multifunctional room, which also serves as a guestroom

2. The kitchen is very simple yet has a very strong presence. The cabinets feature countertops of charcoal granite quartz and are faced in glass, creating bright surfaces that reflect the cityscape. A door leads to the outdoor terrace, which runs the length of the dining room. The very high ceilings were lowered slightly to accommodate lighting fixtures and conceal the electrical controls for the window coverings

3. As a point of departure, space intended for a corridor to one of the penthouses could now be used to house the mechanical and electrical systems. This meant that the apartment could take the form of a great pure rectangle spanning across the full length of the building, with full-height windows on the North, East and West sides that would provide exceptional natural light. The dining room and the adjoining kitchen are at the far North end of the room. The dining room table is surfaced in solid French walnut with a patinated steel base and can seat ten people

138 / 100 Home Design Principles

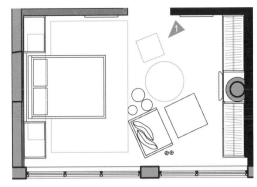

Children Bedroom Plan

1. The son's quarters are in the style of a boutique hotel that has been handled in an almost austere manner. Mostly charcoal, due to the alcove of the bed and the woodwork on the ample storage units, the room has linen curtains and opaque window coverings that can be closed to provide total darkness.This quarter also has a walk-in closet and a bathroom

2. The bedroom of the master of the house is in a rotunda facing due east. Furnishings include a fluted walnut king-sized bed in a charcoal alcove, a long floating walnut chest and two zebra chairs. The hematite curtains can insulate the room from the outer world. The suite includes two walk-in closets and a master bath that has a very refined feeling, with its heated white Calacatta marble floors, the white granite quartz used on the walls, counters and sink, and two curved alcoves finished in gold-leaf tiles with a floral pattern

3. Surrounded by the sky and the ceaselessly changing light from the city beyond, one has the impression of being in a great airborne vessel that provides passengers with all the warmth of a home, yet the freedom of expansive views

33 Flooring's array of time and space

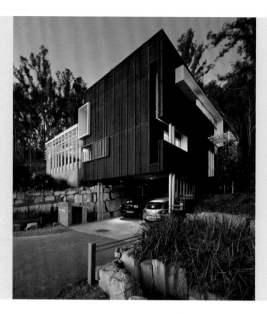

The home interior space design belongs to the four-dimensional plastic arts. When moving in the interior space, one may feel the surroundings with his or her own subjective time concept, experiencing constantly the information in the interior space, both substantial and incorporeal. The floor, as the main interface of the interior space enclosure, reflects clearly the change of the time sequence. Moreover, the light and shadow changes on the ground will rejuvenate the invariable space.

In this case, the designer integrates the living room, the swimming pool and the terrace. When lights come into the room through the grille, the drop shadow makes the open interior space vigorous. The lighting effects that change with time fill the interior space with uncertainty.

Project name: Stonehawke House **Completion date:** 2008 **Location:** Brisbane, Australia **Designer:** Shawn and Natalie Godwin **Photographer:** Christopher Frederick Jones **Area:** 290 sqm

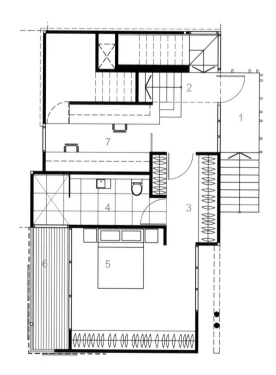

First Floor Plan

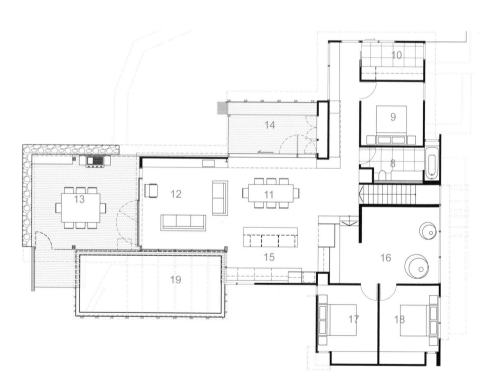

Second Floor Plan

1. External entry	11. Dining
2. Internal entry foyer	12. Living
3. Walk-in robe	13. Deck1
4. Ensuite	14. Deck2
5. Bedroom1	15. Kitchen
6. Private deck	16. Rumpus
7. Study/sewing room	17. Bedroom2
8. Bath	18. Bedroom3
9. Guest	19. Pool
10. Laundry	

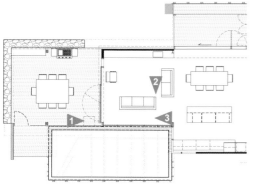

Living+Dining+Kitchen Plan

1. The weaving of light shadow and floor has enhanced the beauty of the sequence in the space

2. Wood textures of the decorative materials go harmoniously with the natural environment

3. Water, wood and light are important decorative elements in the space

1. The blurring high light reflective effects of the floor contrast with the simple and heavy natural environment sharply

2. The reflective effects of the floor have coordinated the style of industrial facilities

3. The texture of the carpet has effectively marked out new functional areas, and soft diffuse effect gives the room a sense of romance and warmth

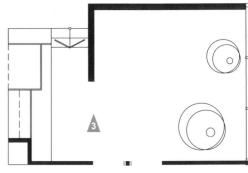

Rumpus Plan

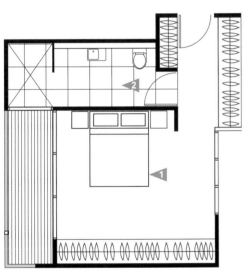

Master Bedroom Plan

1. The matte floor together with the decorative materials of the wall creates a warm environment

2. The multiple diffuse effect of the matt ceramic makes the washroom be more warm and quiet

34 Sinking and rising colours

In home interior space design, the floor, as the foundation of the whole environment, provides all the actual and virtual space with a systematic load-bearing platform. Therefore, the chiaroscuro and changes of warm/cold colour of the floor have a great influence on the whole ambience. The cold colour with low brightness gives people a sinking feeling; the warm colour with high brightness supplies people with a rising feeling.

In this case, the designer chooses a set of space tone with a weak colour contrast. Standing out from the surrounding natural environment, the floor in warm colour with high brightness makes the whole space more transparent and lissome.

Project name: Pryor **Completion date:** 2009 **Location:** New York, USA **Designer:** Bates Masi Architects **Photographer:** Bates Masi Architects **Area:** 297 sqm

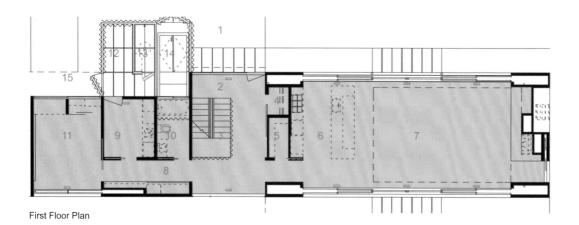

First Floor Plan

1. Entry patio
2. Entry hall
3. Stair
4. Coat closet
5. Pantry
6. Kitchen
7. Living/dining
8. Hall
9. Mudroom
10. Guest bath
11. Guest room
12. Storage
13. Outdoor shower
14. Basement entry
15. Service entry

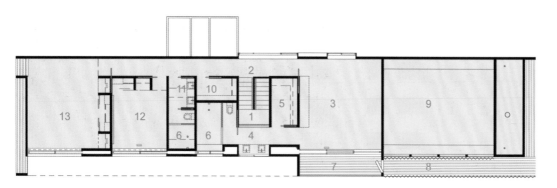

Second Floor Plan

1. Stair
2. Hall
3. Master bedroom
4. Master bath
5. Master closet
6. Shower
7. Balcony
8. Bris soleil
9. Living/dining below
10. Linen closet
11. Bathroom
12. Guest bedroom
13. Kid's bedroom

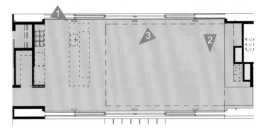

Living Room+Dining Room Plan

1. Multiple layers of bronzed metal fabric at the clerestory windows in the living area fold and unfold to adjust sunlight for optimal brightness & temperature of the space. These operable architectural elements use the natural environment to create suitable living conditions

2. Large glass doors slide open to the living, dining and kitchen area for a large gathering, a smaller scaled swing door for an occasional guest opens to the centre hall with a view of the ocean, and a sequence of auxiliary spaces - beach equipment area, outdoor shower, sand and mudroom - create a seamless ritual from the daily activities for the family and friends

3. The living area, a double height space with kitchen, dining and living area, has thirty-six feet wide glass doors that pocket into southern and northern walls. When open, the dining room becomes a picnic area and the living room fireplace becomes a campfire

Lending to the structure's continuity, the house is assembled, rather than built

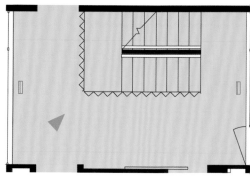

Stair Plan

1. With the owner's initial premise of camping, the design and functionality of the house promote a memorable experience for friends and family in the natural environment

2. The house is environmentally friendly in its overall construction and planning with such specifics as geo-thermal heating & cooling, shading & venting systems, solar panels, organic finishes and materials

3. In all living areas and bedrooms, glass doors and insect screens slide in and out from pocket walls, transforming rooms to screened porches or spaces completely open to the landscape

35 Perspective patterns

In home space design, the designers seldom employ the graphic design to decorate the flooring. They have gradually kept at a distance with the natural organic forms since the Art Nouveau and have chosen the modern style lines that symbolise the speed instead. Though there may still be some eclecticism styles in some post-modern works, the pattern elements have mostly been abstracted.

In this case, the graphic patterns are applied in an uncommon way in that they are used not only on the wall and the roof, but on the floor. The visually perspective changes make the pattern effect on the floor more lively and agile than that on the wall and the roof. The original idea of the designer is to replace the rigid method of putting together all the decorative elements with a flowing decorative style by breaking through the traditional home space design concept.

Project name: River Island **Completion date:** 2010 **Location:** Tokyo, Japan **Designer:** Yusaku Kaneshiro, Hiromi Sato **Photographer:** Masahiro Ishibashi **Area:** 100 sqm

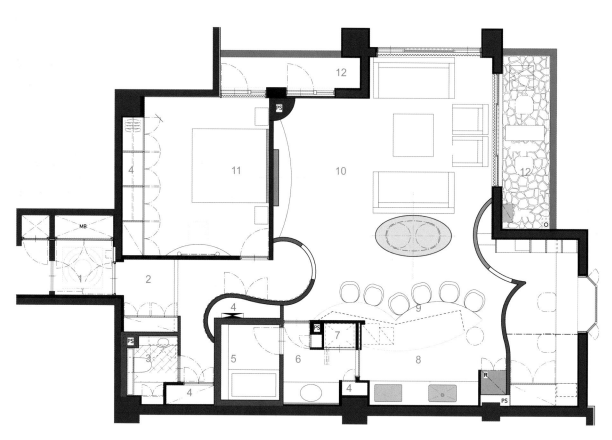

Master Plan

1. Entrance mat	7. Washing machine
2. Entrance	8. Kitchen
3. Bathroom	9. Counter table
4. Closet	10. Living room
5. Bathroom	11. Bedroom
6. Dressing room	12. Veranda

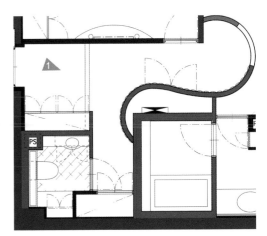

Entrance Plan

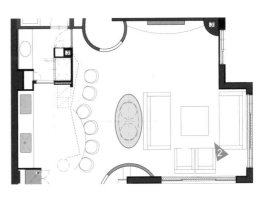

Living Room Plan

2. The private space giving up the concept of "residence" is a decorative space with a gallery-style sense that is an aggregate of forms but combines them together with curves for de-emphasis of themselves

3. Furniture, lighting of the chandelier objects, and wallpaper colour coordination are the elements that complement respective forms and give well-balanced mutual emphasis

1. The exaggerated colours and patterns have greatly enriched this small space

2. The patterns on the floor have made the space be more compacted and cohesive

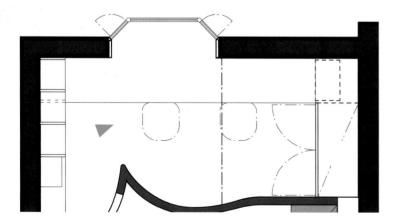

Closet Plan

36 The calm floor

The flooring, as the compositive load-bearing interface, keeps a coordinative composition relationship with the others and furnishing items, which is not only limited to the constitutive relations of the planes but also a harmonious contrast relationship in shape, colour and texture whether from the close-range, medium-range or the long-range perspective.

In this case, the black ground implies a strong weight sense while forming a sharp contrast with the exposed concrete partition wall, the brunet home furnishing and the geometric space modelling.

Project name: Benlaw House **Completion date:** 2010 **Location:** Kuching, Malaysia **Designer:** Design Network Architects **Photographer:** Design Network Architects **Area:** 207 sqm

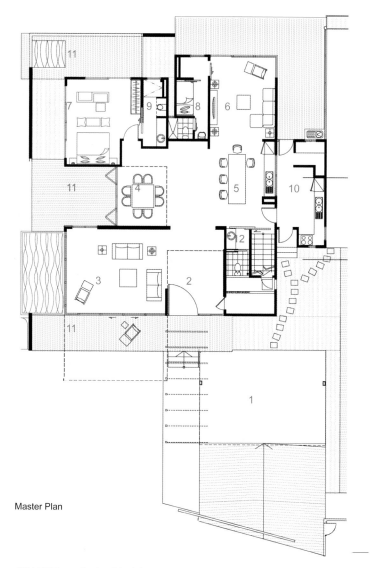

Master Plan

1. Car porch
2. Entrance lobby
3. Living room
4. Dining
5. Dry kitchen
6. Family hall
7. Guest room
8. Utility room
9. Water closet
10. Wet kitchen
11. Timber deck
12. Powder room

1. All the living spaces are then oriented outward to take advantage of the open gardens and water features (and unfortunately also the western sun). As a result of which, screening devices and landscaping are incorporated to create secondary layering screen walls on the ground, to filter sunlight and provide additional privacy

2. The heighten interplay of opposites, the textural against the smooth surfaces, the minimal finish of the white washed rendered wall against the robust concrete shear wall in the living room and the heavy duty black-coated flooring contributes to a subtle consistency of elegant richness and sophistication that comes from refined simplicity

3. Water features provide visual relief and act as an interface for the living space to transit into the garden lawns

4. The house is also raised up higher to restrict view into the living spaces from passersby

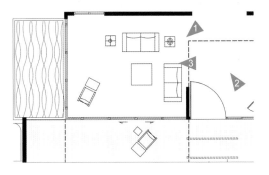

Entrance Lobby+Living Room Plan

5

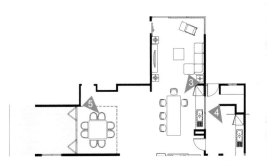

Dining+Dry Kitchen+Family Hall+Wet Kitchen
+Timber Deck Plan

1. The spaces are planned around two voids, created over the main lobby entrance and the dining halls, open and sequential, the social spaces

2. Living/dining/family flow into one another gracefully and spills out into the garden lawn and timber decking

3. The architectural treatment of the first floor is generally solid and more enclosed with large opening placed selectively to capture views while the ground floor is more transparent and open with large glazing all round, maximising on the fluidity between the inside and outside

4. The clients coordinated much of the construction hands on and were involved in the final fitting out of the interior design with the diligent help of the contractor on site. And as you probably guessed, they did the kitchen installation

5. Finishes are pare down and worked on with only a minimal palette. The honest expression of materials and even sometimes, the crudeness of the constructional workmanship are deliberately highlighted. The chipped edges, the scars on the walls, the unfinished floor with the slight dent are tolerated and incorporated in as part of the design as if intentional

37 The pleasure of fixed pattern of vision

In home interior space design, the wall, as the principal part of the enclosure interface, can endow people with a stable feeling of being enclosed. The observational habituation of people lead them to focus more of their attentions on the shape, colour and texture of the wall, as a result, the visual effects of the wall play a significant role in influencing the whole spatial ambience. Modern interior design tends to pay more attention to the relationship between the structure, the scale and the proportion with less concentration on the detail design. The image of the wall needs to be taken into consideration with the overall composition of the space.

In this case, the material chosen for the wall with simple design keeps coordinative with the scale and proportion of the whole space, thus enjoying a distinct sense of space. The colour and the shape of the wall have undergone the complanation and merged into the whole environment.

Project name: ViGi House **Completion date:** 2010 **Location:** Villa Gading Indah, Kelapa Gading, Jakarta, Indonesia **Designer:** Edy Hartono, Edha Architects **Photographer:** Fernando Gomulya from Techtography **Area:** 378 sqm

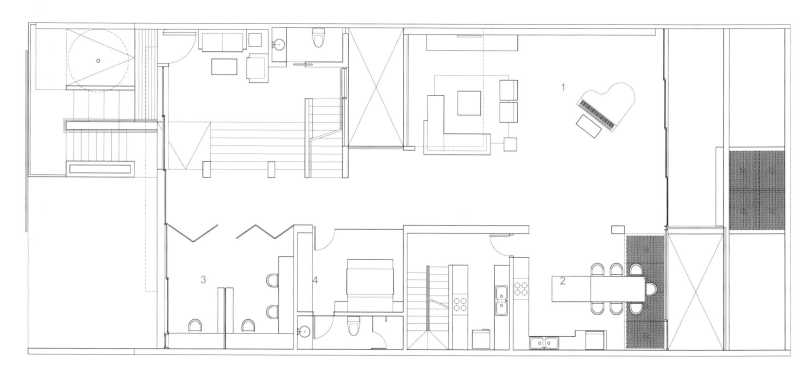

Second Floor Plan

1. Living room
2. Dining space
3. Study room
4. Sub-bedroom/servant's bed room

1. Beside the opening to the common carp pond and the backyard, there's also an opening to the void and living room. This creates a harmony sustainability of architectural language

2. In the study room, there is transparent and flexible folding door. So that when it's opened, giving such wider area impression and unified between the study room itself, the corridor, and the foyer

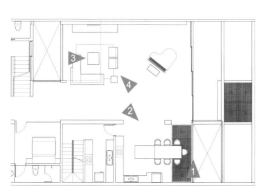

Living Room+Dining Space Plan

1. The unified area could also be found between the living room, pantry and the dining room which oriented to the backyard and the common carp pond

2. Using glass as material for the floor in the dining room and pantry area, to create interactions between the dry garden and mini bar area below

3. With the skylight along the dining room to the living room, plus the maximum openings, these all create shading to the interior organisation of the living room. And also with the existence of the simple architectural detail at the common carp pond, all of them present a very well integrated space composition and creating a comprehensive architectural dialogue which result richness of space visual aesthetic

4. Sensation of movement, both horizontally and vertically, is felt because of the dynamism as the result of that interaction

38 The segmentation and combination of the wall

In home interior space design, the segmentation and combination of the wall is mainly to meet the requirements of the space subdivision besides satisfying the demand of the formal composition. The classic separation ratio will enhance the space hierarchy and the visual joyfulness.

In this case, the designer, successfully combining modern design technique with Chinese traditional culture, makes consolidated improvement to the traditional living environment and style and the decorative material, especially in the living room where the designer designs the enclosed wall above the patio as a bookshelf. The decorative sign with a strong cultural sense demonstrates successfully the spatial ambience and the client's taste.

Project name: Villa No.10 **Completion date:** 2010 **Location:** Shanghai, China **Designer:** MoHen Design International/Hank M.Chao **Photographer:** MoHen Design International/ Maoder Chou **Area:** 430 sqm **Materials:** marble, cassia siamea, oak, stone, silver foil, iron, stainless steel, pearl board

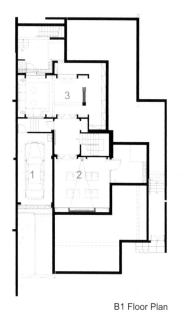

B1 Floor Plan

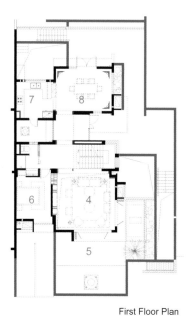

First Floor Plan

Second Floor Plan

Third Floor Plan

1. Garage
2. Media room
3. Family room
4. Living room
5. Garden
6. Bedroom1
7. Kitchen
8. Dining room
9. Bedroom2
10. Master bathroom
11. Study room
12. Master bedroom

1. The bealock-like wall makes the space be more spacious

2. The decorative mirror at the corner of wall visually enhances the deep sense of the space

3. As to the living room, designer brought in the concept of "a depositary of Buddhist texts", not only designer made something in the high ceiling, some bookshelves in between the mezzanine section, and the overlap of the bridge as a way to connect the docking space. The living room is also leading into some kind of knowledge environment

4. From a logical and historical point of view, designer has always been very curious about what kind of thing exactly should be from Chinese style to the current 21st century. Of course, some of the old Chinese styles are not comfortable, materials are not durable, and some of other weak points should be totally avoided or modified for sure. On the contrary, there are always some inherent characteristics of Chinese style, the depth and level of landscaping on certain spaces, and the use of simple repetition on elements. These advantages should be retained or even further enhanced. Based on this logic structure, it becomes the fundamental design concepts and principles for this villa project

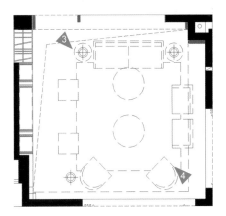

Living Room Plan

1. It is better to open up the space of bar and wine cellar for more layering feeling and won't appear to be narrow
2. The function of the basement is mainly to meet the master's needs for entertainment
3. A large living room combines its possession of liquor and goods and receiving functions
4. The other side of the master bedroom is master's internal study room which directly connecting to the master bathroom

Recreation Room Plan

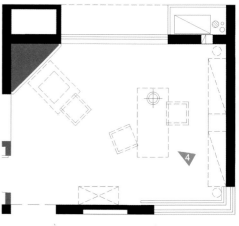

Study Room Plan

1. For the background of the master bed designer used shell plate positioning to emphasise its own specificity

2. Designer decorated the entrance of the changing room with the Carp Traditional Chinese painting to make a dull door into an opaque paint

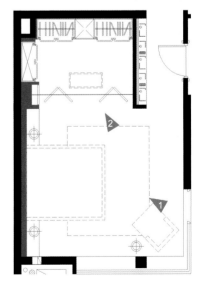

Master Bedroom Plan

39 The extension of vision

In home interior space design, designers' concepts may sometimes be subject to many limits, namely, the structure of the building, the clients' requirements and the budget. Even so, to avoid or cope with these restrictions, the designers are always able to find one or several proper approaches, among which the most typical example is the breakthrough in wall design that indicates clearly the designers' appeal. The wall, as the leading enclosure interface, assumes lots of integrated specialities. The directivity of the wall represents directly the mobility of the space.

In this case, the designer builds a set of mobile spaces for the client, a fashion designer. All the spaces from the workroom at the entrance to the master bedroom are full of the flowing curve elements. The changing curve geometry of the wall shows people clearly the directions and reflects visually the living condition of the client.

Project name: Private Apartment - New Westgate Garden **Completion date:** 2010 **Location:** Shanghai, China **Designer:** Dariel and Arfeuillere – A Lime 388 Company **Photographer:** Tristan Chapuis **Area:** 150 sqm

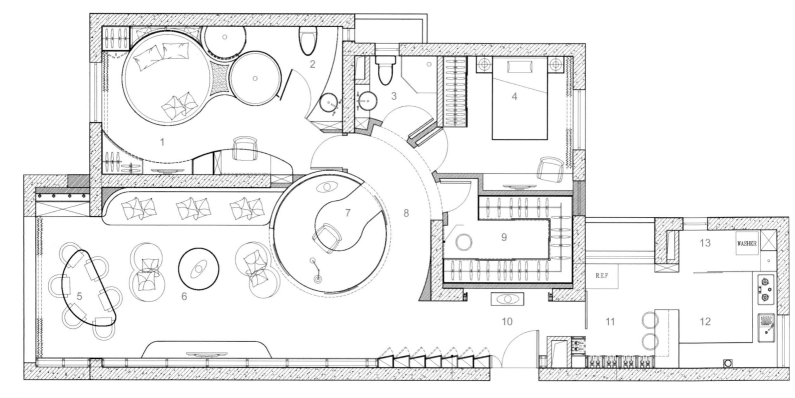

Master Plan

1. Master bedroom	8. Corridor
2. Toilet	9. Closet
3. Toilet	10. Vestibule
4. Guest bedroom	11. Bar area
5. Dining room	12. Kitchen
6. Living room	13. Work room
7. Studio	

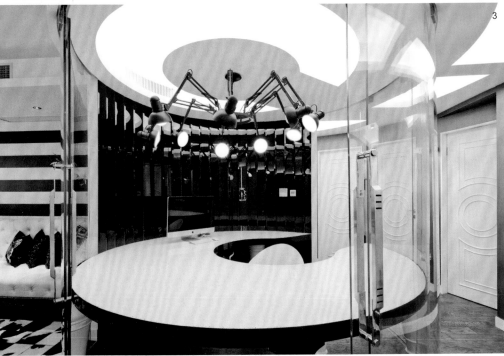

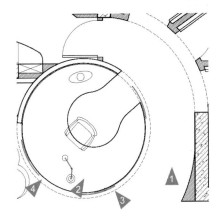

1. The corridor organised around a central working area highlights the space and reminds the creativity of its inhabitant. Curves and soft lines convey elegance and poesy while large black and white stripes give a vivid POP feeling

2. For this apartment, the designers had to consider the personality and the needs, personal as well as professional, of their client, a fashion designer

3. This room is one of the key innovations of the designers for which they created a round and transparent space made of a special glass and a curved glossy working table following perfectly the shape of the cover

4. The study area allows the hostess to stay connected with the rest of the apartment while offering her a private nest to concentrate on her work

Corridor+Studio Plan

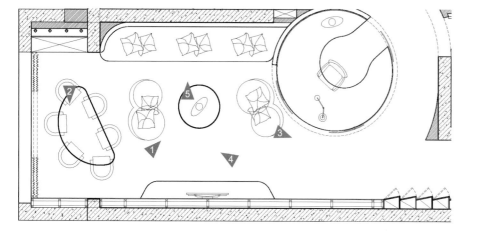

1. The living room designed to be the heart of the apartment is built upon two communicating spaces. While the first part is a classy and romantic reception the other space displays a futuristic transparent study created so that the hostess could have her own working area without dedicating a separate and closed room to it

2. Everything from the materials they used to the tailored furniture perfectly oozes style and charm

3. Overall the designers have played between the elegance of black and white elements and a romantic usage of pink to match the client personality

4. In the reception area a series of black and white pieces of furniture such as the over length leather sofa, the white lacquered ellipse table and its matching chairs are creating an atmosphere of luxury and romance

5. The pieces are echoing to the black and white stripped arc shaped background wall and a matching printed cow rug to bring class and elegance to the entire space

Living Room+Dining Room Plan

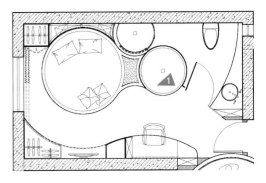

Master Bedroom Plan

1. Butterflies that can also be found on the cushions of the living room sofa are the best symbol of the owner personality. Their romantic and feminine feeling is the key inspiration for this utmost private space that is the main bedroom

2. Everything from the soft touch of the carpet, the vivid pink and the round bed and bathtub are a deliberate tribute to air, lightness and poesy. A game of curves and colours from the dresser to the washroom mirror contribute to the magic feeling of the space

40 The gradation of the vertical

In home interior space design, the wall and the large furnishings enrich the vertical space dimension. The shape of the wall changes with the space changes and unifies with the space unification. The elements such as the shape, scale, colour and texture are all important means to enrich the wall hierarchy.

In this case, the designer applies the modern decorative technique by choosing the black and white colour as the keynote of the space. The colour and shape of the wall match up perfectly with the overall space configuration with rich hierarchy and striking contrast.

Project name: Adria 2-Bedroom Showflat **Completion date:** 2010 **Location:** 21 Derbyshire Road, Singapore **Designer:** ONG&ONG Pte Ltd **Photographer:** See Chee Keong

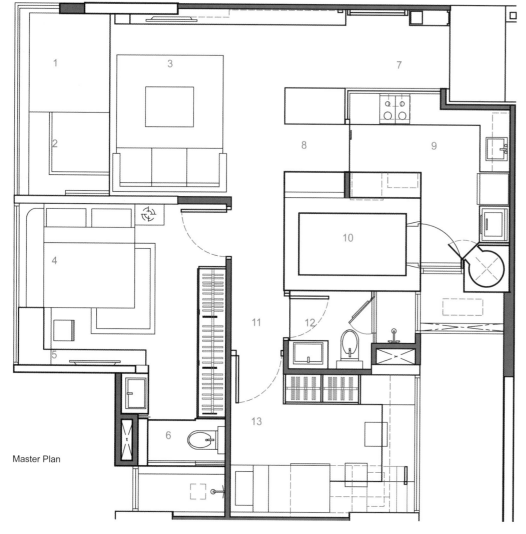

Master Plan

1. Balcony
2. Outdoor dining
3. Living room
4. Master bedroom
5. Study
6. Master bathroom
7. Foyer
8. Dry kitchen
9. Kitchen
10. Store room
11. Corridor
12. Common bathroom
13. Bedroom2

1. Monochromatic tones stylishly present each space within dark walls, contrasted against white Volakas marble floor

2. Communal areas are compact yet luxurious with the fusion of kitchen, living and dining rooms. This seamless transition between areas gives the apartment an impression of greater space

3. Simple linear elements create interesting perspectives, while mirrors are cleverly employed to enhance the apartment's depth

4. The kitchen is well appointed with simple yet elegant white cabinets that create a clean, modern canvas

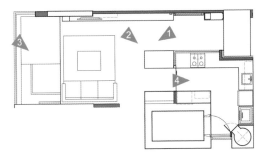

Kitchen+Living Room Plan

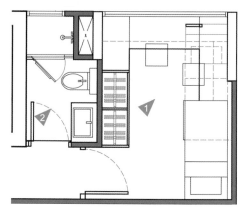

Bedroom 2 Plan

1. A funny layered bunk bed and glass study desk create an amazing space
2. These apartments demonstrate simplicity at its best

1

2

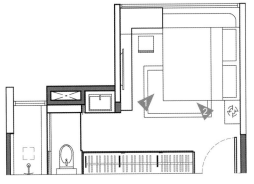

Master Bedroom Plan

1. The project embodies the sophisticated modernity of city life
2. While a dramatic stone wall in the master bedroom serves as a key visual element

41 The tactile sense of texture

In home interior space design, the texture of the wall influences directly men's perception of the texture of the whole space. People's perception of the interior environment belongs to the four-dimensional process, but the changes in wall details can always be the foothold of human emotions. The changes in detail make people know the surroundings better and integrate themselves into the whole environment more easily.

In this case, the designer highlights the classic and eternal design motif by the collocation of different materials, setting up a spiritual paradise in the noisy city.

Project name: The Ritz-Carlton Residences at MahaNakhon **Completion date:** 2010 **Location:** Bangkok, Thailand **Designer:** David Collins Studio **Photographer:** Richard Powers Photography **Area:** 410 sqm

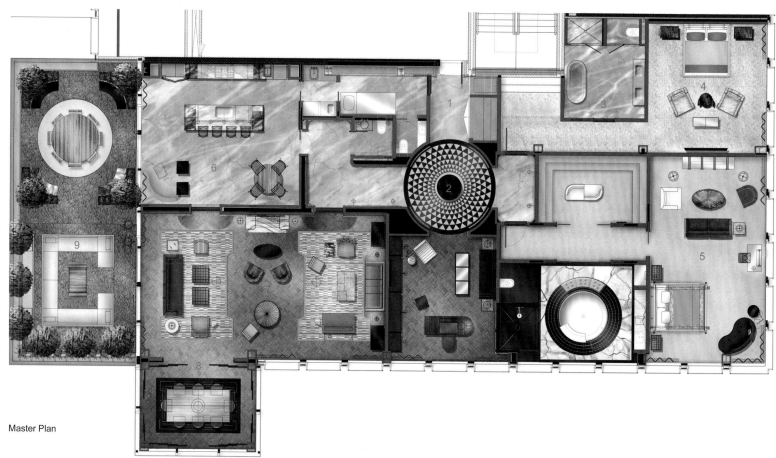

Master Plan

1. Entrance lobby
2. Corridor leading from entrance lobby to living room
3. Guest bathroom
4. Guestroom
5. Master bedroom
6. Kitchen
7. Living room
8. Dining room
9. Floating garden

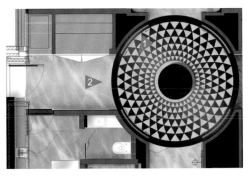

Entrance Lobby Plan

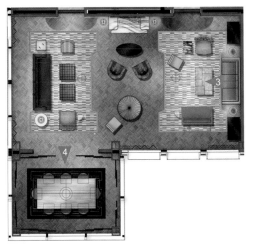

Living Room+Dining Room Plan

1. Silver travertine and black marble floor

2. The designers have taken the idea of 21st Century living and imbued it with energy, whilst at the same time keeping it grounded in classical vocabulary making it timeless

3. The living room is made up of several conversation areas- clusters of bespoke furniture pieces, silk velvet rugs, timber flooring, and customised intimate lighting - an adaptable space for modern entertaining or simple contemplation

4. It is designed as a haven from this busy and exciting city. This is an elegantly proportioned interior, which captures, in essence, the importance of the most valuable luxury - time and space, inspired by the grandeur of generations of historic stately Manhattan apartment homes from the time of the Vanderbilts, the Astors and the Whitneys

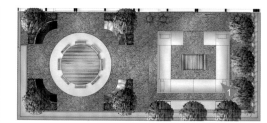

Floating Garden Plan

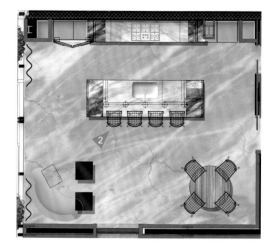

Kitchen Plan

1. The floating garden will be an oasis of calm, with water as its central element the interpretation of a Thai garden

2. The design concept derives from many years of refining a concept called "minimalist luxury". The style is focused on the importance of detail, colour, atmosphere, lighting and comfort

Master Bedroom Plan

1. This will be like a home in a building, exclusive, grand, sumptuous and luxurious but contemporary
2. The bathrooms offer the ultimate in luxury for pampering and relaxation – a sanctuary
3. This is an iconic building which will make its all-important debut on the Bangkok skyline. This is Bangkok city living at its most prestigious

42 Flowing decorations

In home interior space design, only the natural lighting effect can change with time, demonstrating a kind of decorative uncertainty. How the wall can receive and reflect the lights depends on the volume of the light and the texture of the wall. The multiple reflection between the contiguous walls can increase the space hierarchy and texture.

In this case, the designer brings in the natural light in large areas and achieves the gentler colour transition and the richer hierarchy through the wall shape design and the exquisite texture changes on the wall surface.

Project name: 45 Faber Park **Completion date:** 2009 **Location:** Singapore city, Singapore **Designer:** ONG&ONG Pte Ltd **Photographer:** Derek Swalwell, Tim Nolan **Area:** 592 sqm

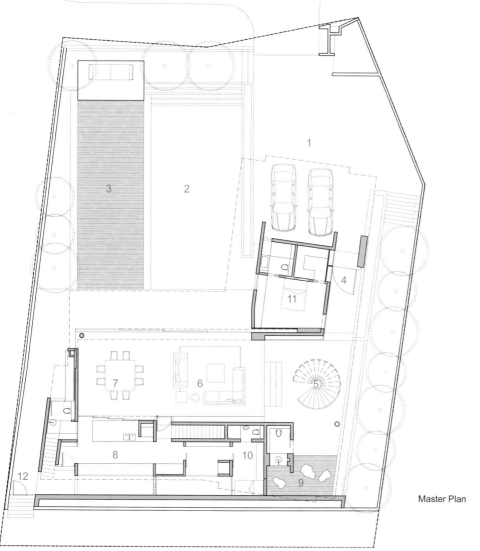

Master Plan

1. Carpark
2. Garden
3. Pool
4. Entrance
5. Hall
6. Living room
7. Dining room
8. Kitchen
9. Yard
10. Service room
11. Guest bedroom
12. Rear entrance

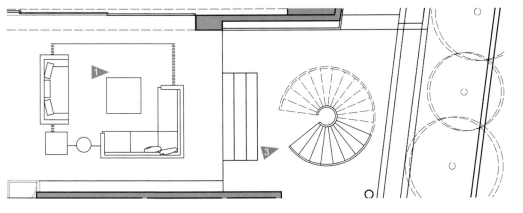

Living Room Plan

1. The overall concept, derived from the clients' requirements, was to create a living space open to the outdoors in a clean contemporary aesthetic

2. The building would need to allow fluid movement between each space within and perform as a sustainable mechanism

3. Under the effect of the light and shade, the texture of façade changes with the changes of shape

In order to maximise space, the idea of pushing the mass of the building into the corner of the plot was developed

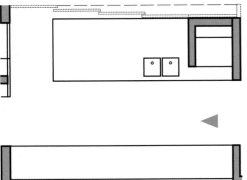

Kitchen Plan

1. The reflection and diffusion of the natural light together with various façade textures has enriched the space visually

2. The soft lighting changes have strengthened the quiet atmosphere

3. The materials, chosen in subtle tones, define and reflect the more intimate space of the house. The arrangement of spaces is a functional response to the needs of the inhabitants. In response to this, what the spaces created were introspective and focused on privacy

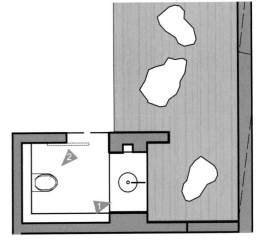

Guest Bedroom Plan

43 The keynote of space

There are many ways to set the keynote of the home interior space. Different standards may give birth to different effects, while the colour change of the wall is an intuitive way to form the space tone. As the main enclosure interface of the interior space, the wall enjoys the most area of colour coverage. The colour change of the wall can provide a consulting platform for other decorative elements including the home furnishings.

In this case, the designer, using the stone walls in warm grey and the wood veneer in ocher colour as the decorative material of the wall, together with the client's artworks display, creates the interior environment with the characteristics of the Classicism.

Project name: California Residence **Completion date:** 2010 **Location:** Los Angeles, USA **Designer:** Landry Design Group **Photographer:** Erhard Pfeiffer **Area:** 12,000 sqm

1. A palette of warm grey limestone and richly stained woods form the basis for the interior of the home

2. Pocketing glass door systems blur the distinction between indoors and out, while providing the necessary protection for the couple's extensive contemporary art collection

1. Whether entertaining a large group of friends or spending a quiet evening with their three children the communal spaces of the home remain intimate and inviting

2. Accents of copper, Pennsylvania bluestone, specialty glass, and bronze detailing added interest

3. Blending the residence with the natural landscape and incorporating the clients' way of life has allowed the home to take full advantage of its site

4. Materials were chosen not only for their natural beauty and durability but also to compliment the artwork

5. A refreshing personal expression of the family's values and lifestyle has been achieved

44 The continuity of the vision

In home interior space design, the wall shape plays an important role in visual guidance. The open and even wall can lead people's sight to move around the space, thus forming the complete space experience soon. On the contrary, the wall shape with diversified details may always make people's sight stagnated. Only by the implication of the details can one appreciate the spatial ambience.

In this case, the designer designs the walls into a unified interface with extremely simple shape and colour. Under the guidance of the strong sense of straight lines, people's vision may be extended to the whole space.

Project name: 870 UN Plaza **Completion date:** 2007 **Location:** New York, USA **Designer:** Andre Kikoski Architect **Photographer:** Frank Oudeman **Area:** 418 sqm

Master Plan

1. Vestibule/entry	7. Kitchen
2. Foyer & stair	8. Den
3. Library bar	9. Bathroom
4. Library	10. Laundry room
5. Living room	11. Powder room
6. Dining room	12. Elevator

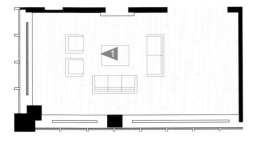

Living Room Plan

1. The pure white walls and the open floating window form a flowing visual experience

2. Circular stair set against a wall of leather-wrapped panels and extensive use of American Black Walnut millwork are just a few of the elegant custom finishes

3. The exceptional materials and careful consideration of details distinguish it in this modernist tower

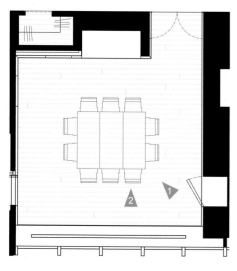

Dining Room Plan

1. With its commanding views from every room, the apartment is a natural for grand and intimate entertaining. The designer highlights this attribute and emphasises gracious daily living as well. The vertical separating lines echo with the checkerboard on the dining-table, reflecting the spatial characteristics of lightness. The edge lines of the frame continue this intuitive visual experience

2. The combination of these sophisticated materials and superior craftsmanship create a soft and elegant modernism in fulfillment of the owner's vision for the space

3. The colour and texture of the background wall have organised the home furnishings orderly

1. The apartments are notable mostly for their large and tall windows and views

2. The sumptuous textures and material palette are unique and understated. They distinguish the apartment for visitors, but also enhance the residents' everyday experiences

3. The mirror reflection effect has expanded the space visually, giving a new continuation of the vision

45 The background of space

In home interior space design, the enclosure effect of the wall defines the whole spatial ambience. The other interfaces and furnishings dress up the space on the basis of the shape and form of the wall. Ultimately, the wall image completely integrates into the overall space configuration.

In this case, the designer sets a unified tone for the interior space through the overall treatment effect of the wall, creating the elegant and tranquil spatial ambience in cooperation with the ground and the home furnishings.

Project name: Adria 3-Bedroom Apartments **Completion date:** 2007 **Location:** Singapore City, Singapore **Designer:** ONG&ONG Pte Ltd **Photographer:** See Chee Keong **Area:** 274 sqm

Master Plan

1. Balcony	9. Kitchen	17. Gallery
2. Outdoor dining	10. Store room	18. Balcony
3. Living room	11. Corridor	19. Entertainment room
4. Master bedroom	12. Common bathroom	20. Eating area
5. Study	13. Bedroom2	21. Powder room
6. Master bathroom	14. Wet Kitchen	22. Office
7. Foyer	15. Yard	23. Equipment room
8. Dry kitchen	16. Grand living area	

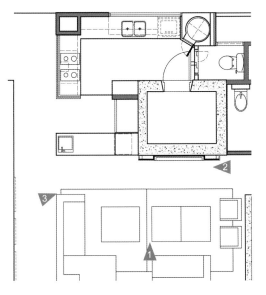

Living Room+Kitchen+Entertainment Room Plan

1. The kitchen, the living and the dining rooms exist as a continuous space, each unconstrained by partitions

2. The spacious living room and balcony is a unified, multi-purpose area. A full height, glass display shelf demarcates an additional activity area, and this provides an exhibition space without compromising the feeling of openness

3. The communal areas are compact yet luxurious with the fusion of kitchen, living and dining rooms. This seamless transition between areas gives the apartment an impression of greater space. The kitchen is well appointed with simple yet elegant white cabinets that create a clean, modern canvas

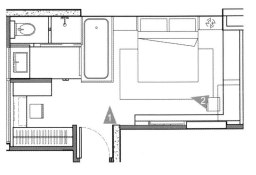

Master Bedroom+Master Bathroom Plan

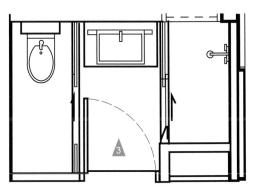

Common Bathroom Plan

1. The glass seamlessly links the two spaces as an aesthetic whole
2. In the master bedroom, warm-coloured marble runs uninterruptedly into the glass partitioned bathroom

46 New echo

In home interior space design, the scale and proportion exert the most obvious influence over the sense of space. The space can become wider or smaller by changing the shape and the height of the ceiling.

In this case, the designer takes the ceiling design of the living room, the study and the dining room and the building structure together into consideration while bringing in the natural light into the interior space. Through the large scale window on the rooftop, the designer makes the natural light the important decorative elements of the interior space. However, it is the client's demand that gives birth to the inspiration of the design which expresses the client's optimistic and positive values and lifestyle.

Project name: Basin Ledge **Completion date:** 2008 **Location:** Austin, USA **Designer:** Dick Clark Architecture **Photographer:** Dick Clark Architecture **Area:** 622 sqm

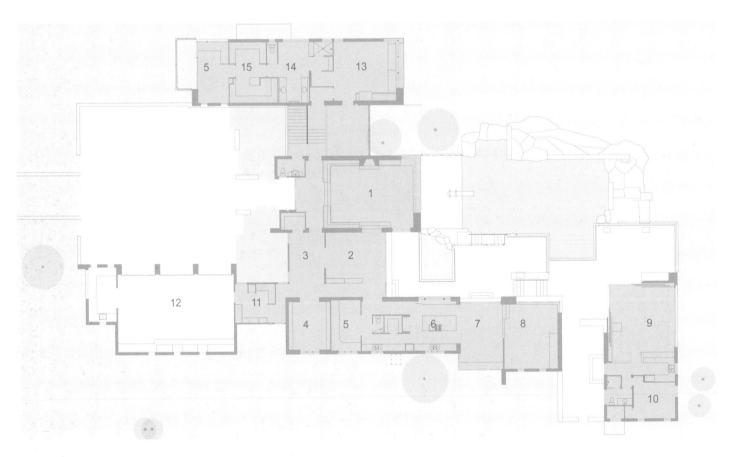

Master Plan

1. Living	6. Kitchen	11. Mudroom
2. Formal dining	7. Dining	12. Garage
3. Entry hall	8. Den	13. Master bed
4. Library	9. Pool house	14. Master bath
5. Study room	10. Guest quarters	15. Master closet

1. Lighting in this design becomes an important component to build the colourful interior. Inspired by the clients' desire to live in a house that reflects their values and lifestyle, the house takes an architecturally minimal approach with simple massing, an understated material palette, and large expanses of glass

2. Configured for entertainment, the glass box living area, along with large sliding doors from the dining and pool room invites guests outside onto the pool deck to take in the spectacular view of the Austin skyline

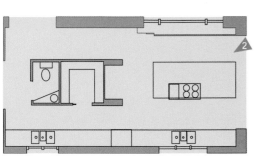

Dining Room Plan

1. Minimalist furniture with red, black and gold colours are arranged in good combination

2. Ivory colour dominates the interior and gives clean impression

3. The design brings together traditional and contemporary forms and textures to create a home with welcoming spaces

47 The restriction of space

In home interior design, the ceiling's restriction to the interior space represent the condition of close and flowing. The closed ceiling thoroughly isolates the interior space from the exterior while the transparent roof can integrate the interior and the exterior space, dimming the space boundary.

In this case, the designer designs the roof into a transparent interface, which maintains the integrity of the three-dimensional space and the fluidity of various spaces in both the horizontal and the vertical directions and moreover brings in the landscape elements from the exterior space.

Project name: Cetatuia Loft **Completion date:** 2009 **Location:** Brasov, Romania **Designer:** Ion Popusoi, Bogdan Preda **Photographer:** Cosmin Dragomir **Area:** 1500 sqm

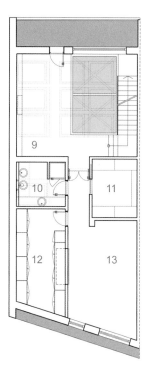

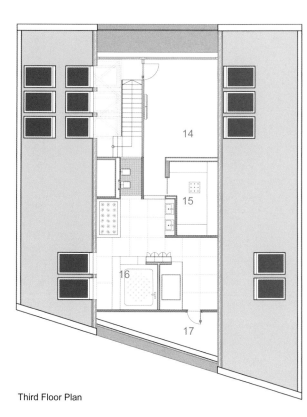

First Floor Plan

Second Floor Plan

Third Floor Plan

1. Entry hall
2. Living room
3. Dining room
4. Kitchen
5. Bathroom
6. WC
7. Technical space
8. Office

9. Fireplace
10. Bathroom
11. Storage
12. Dressing
13. Bedroom

14. Bedroom
15. Bedroom
16. Bathroom
17. Technical space

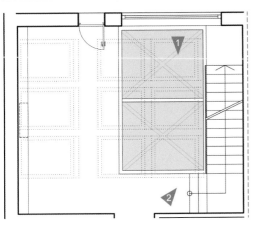

1. Without these glazed surfaces – horizontal and vertical – the house would have lost a very important spatial dimension and the relationship between the interior and the landscape

2. Railing was almost dematerialised by transparent glass, thus non-essential elements that altered the clear perception of the space where eliminated as much as possible. The stair was reduced to its minimum – the steps

3. Windows reach to the floor, which makes the room appear larger, flooded with light, while roof windows bring daylight deep down into the living room through the glass flooring

Fireplace Plan

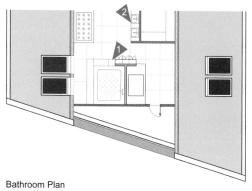

Bathroom Plan

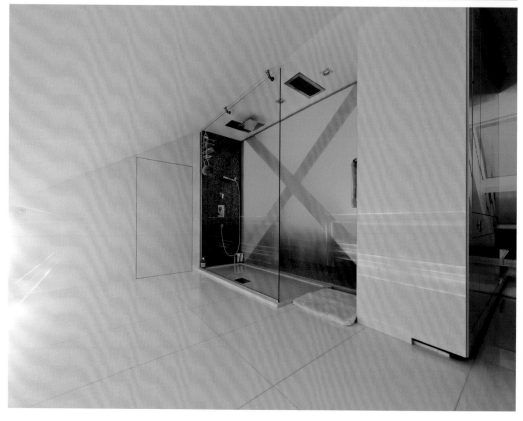

1. The glass wall on the top floor for the master's bedroom opens a new direction to the living room

2. The glass wall farther to the city through the roof windows

48 The hint of thinking

In home interior space design, the continuity and directivity of the roof intuitively imply the spatial direction and the routes of people's activities. Meanwhile, the ceiling shape can convey dynamic rhythm of the four-dimensional space through the arrangement of arrays, which plays a key role in creating the active spatial ambience.

In this case, the designer breaks the traditional mode of construction: adopt the treatment of elevation by using the French window to increase interactivity while arranging the wooden beams successively in arrays in the spatial direction to increase the sense of depth of the space in terms of the ceiling treatment of the public space on the first floor.

Project name: Cabin GJ-5 **Completion date:** 2008 **Location:** Lillestrom, Norway **Designer:** Architect Gudmundur Jonsson **Photographer:** Jiri Havran **Area:** 156 sqm

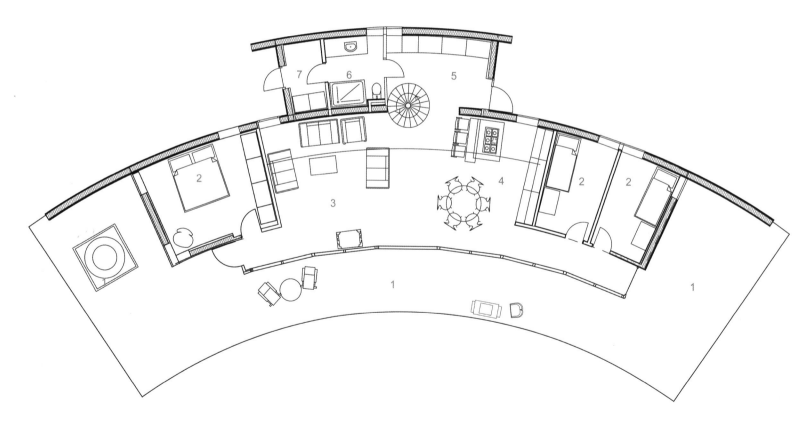

First Floor Plan

1. Veranda	5. Entrance
2. Bedroom	6. Bathroom
3. Living room	7. Laundry
4. Kitchen	

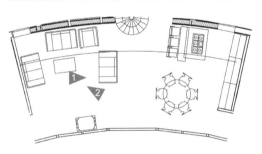

Living Room Plan

1. The Norwegian landscape is beautiful and it is a pity not being able to visually experience the scenery from the inside of the cabins due to the lack of windows and the sizes of them. Designer's reaction resulted in a totally glazed front of the cabin facing the view. In order to being able to encounter the view together with the fireplace, which is located by the floor-to-ceiling windows. The design of ceiling implies the fluidity of the space

2. This cabin is a modern reaction to the old Norwegian cabin-tradition

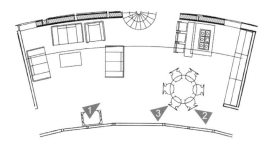

Living Room+ Kitchen+Dining Plan

1. The cabin has a clear division in zones divided by the curved main wall, in front the living room, kitchen/dining and bedrooms and at the backside the entrance and technical part

2. The curved form embraces nature and the curve acts as a cross-stabilisor as well

3. The top chandeliers defined the dining area

The organisation of stone and wood has created a natural space environment

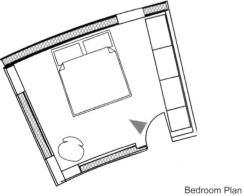

Bedroom Plan

49 The overall coordination

In home interior space design, the designing style of the ceiling should conform to the space form, the whole spatial style and the regional division of different functional areas. According to the requirements of the whole space configuration, the roof design, as the auxiliary interface, can assist the wall and the ground design to make the space integrate and open. Meanwhile, the ceiling design can also work with other interior in their contrastive and harmonious relations to be the leading role of the space decoration.

In this case, the designer chooses the uniform flat ceiling designing style to make the whole space simple and open while highlighting the other surfaces and furnishings.

Project name: House Engen **Completion date:** 2009 **Location:** Oslo, Norway **Designer:** Dahle & Breitenstein AS Christian Dahle and Kurt Breitenstein **Photographer:** Nils Petter Dale **Area:** 356 sqm

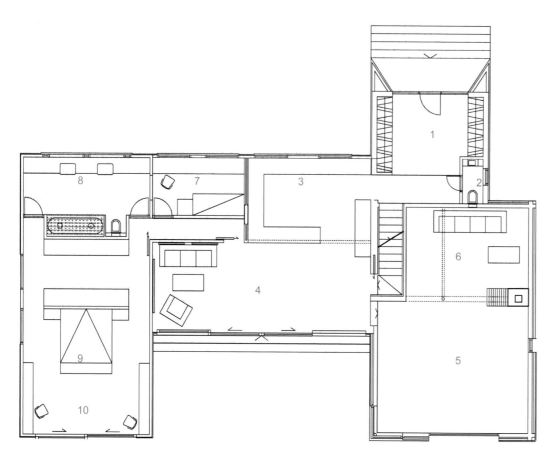

1. Entrance
2. WC
3. Kitchen
4. Dining room
5. Living room
6. Library with fire place
7. Guest/office
8. Master bathroom
9. Master wardrobe
10. Master bedroom

First Floor Plan

The entrance body is the only really new elements to the building. It contrasts the modesty of the old hose all though it plays along both in material and in shape. Where the existing entrance was - in due of all the stages it was buildt - hidden in an awkward corner, the new entrance wishes welcome. It inverts the old ceiling and opens up for visitors, giving a glimpse of what's inside

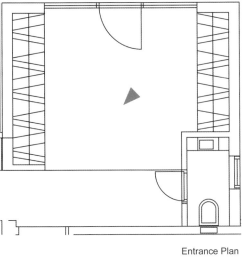

Entrance Plan

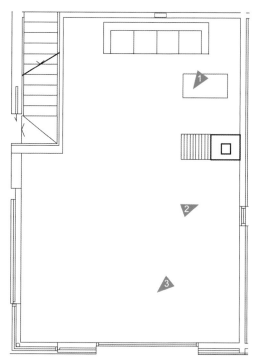

Living Room Plan

1. With a mirroring of the stairs the sections follow up the new transformed circulation to a dynamic flow of space, but also enable room for contemplation. Simple top design goes through different functional areas within the living room, coordinating the different atmospheres in the space perfectly

2. The house has kept its traditional Norwegian wooden house character and still has something contemporary

3. Simple top design naturally attracts the attention onto the art and garden

The west wing is like a house on its own with a master bedroom with a view to the garden and the swimming pool

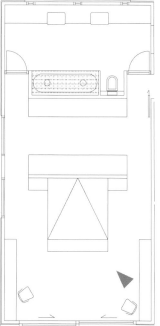

Master Bedroom Plan

50   The forgotten face

In home interior space design, the roof materials, restricted by their own weight and the difficulties of construction, are in fewer varieties than the other interfaces. In addition, the habitual observing manner from the bottom to the top of people makes the roof design an auxiliary part of the whole interior design. If we can jump out of the restrictions of the material and shape, the roof image will produce a strong tensile force visually.

In this case, the designer chooses the wood with digitalised engraved patterns as the main decorative material of the roof. The structure in streamline shape intensifies the dynamic effect of the whole space. The designer aims to make a visual contrast with the traditional Hawaii woodcarving in this way and moreover modernise the tradition form through digitalised sculpting techniques.

Project name: Kona Residence **Completion date:** 2010 **Location:** Kona, Hawaii **Designer:** Hagy Belzberg **Photographer:** Benny Chan (Fotoworks), Belzberg Architects **Area:** 725 sqm

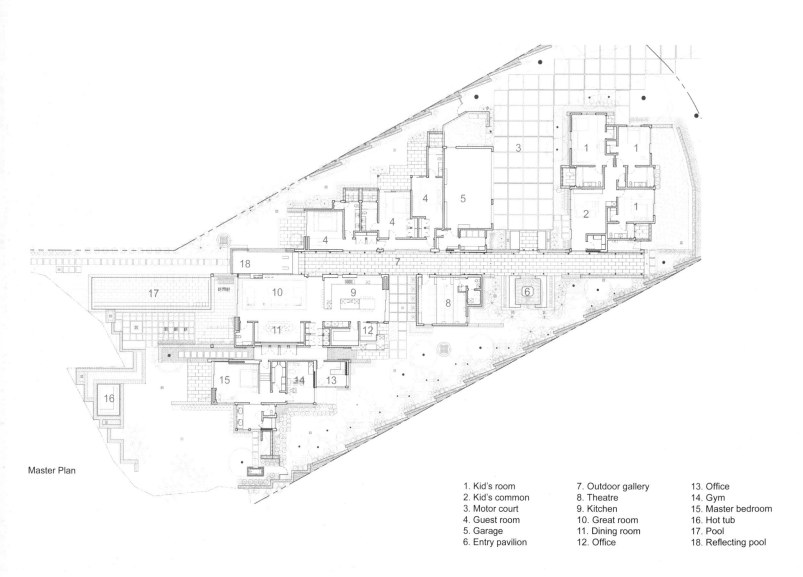

Master Plan

1. Kid's room	7. Outdoor gallery	13. Office
2. Kid's common	8. Theatre	14. Gym
3. Motor court	9. Kitchen	15. Master bedroom
4. Guest room	10. Great room	16. Hot tub
5. Garage	11. Dining room	17. Pool
6. Entry pavilion	12. Office	18. Reflecting pool

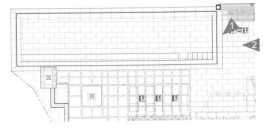

Pool Plan

1. To help maintain the environmental sensitivity of the house, two separate arrays of roof-mounted photovoltaic panels offset the residence energy usage while the choice of darker lava stone helped heat the pool water via solar radiation

2. Within the dichotomy of natural elements and a geometric hardscape, the residence attempts to integrate both the surrounding views of volcanic mountain ranges to the east and ocean horizons westward

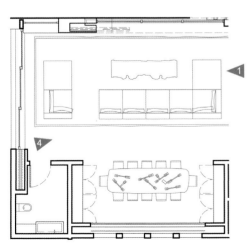

1. Various digitally sculpted wood ceilings and screens, throughout the house, continue the abstract approach to traditional Hawaiian wood carving further infusing traditional elements into the contemporary arrangement

2. Living area and lap pool corner

3. Details of wood ceiling

4. Antonio Citterio sectionals rest on a custom coloured Andree Putman rug in the living area

Living Room Plan

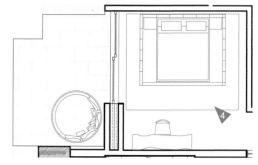

Guset Room Plan

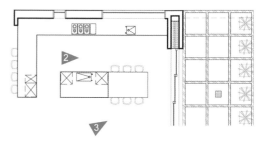

Kitchen+Dining Room Plan

2/3. The programme is arranged as a series of pods distributed throughout the property, each having its own unique features and view opportunities

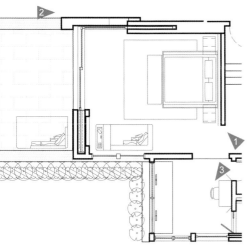

Master Bedroom Plan

4. The decorative mosaic wall

51 The imagination of space

In home interior space design, lighting on the top surface is used more often as the auxiliary decorative light source than as the main illuminant of the interior space. The combination lighting systems such as the down lamp, reflector lamp, pendant lamp, ceiling lamp and the electroluminescent lamp not only magnify the luminous effect on the top surface, but enrich people's emotional experience in the whole interior space.

In this case, the designer adopts various kinds of comprehensive ceiling lighting systems matched up with large-scale furniture and open French windows to make the interior space much wider. The fictitious space has been divided in restrictive ways.

Project name: Floating House **Completion date:** 2009 **Location:** Seoul, South Korea **Designer:** Hyunjoon Yoo Architects **Photographer:** Hyunjoon Yoo Architects **Area:** 195.52 sqm

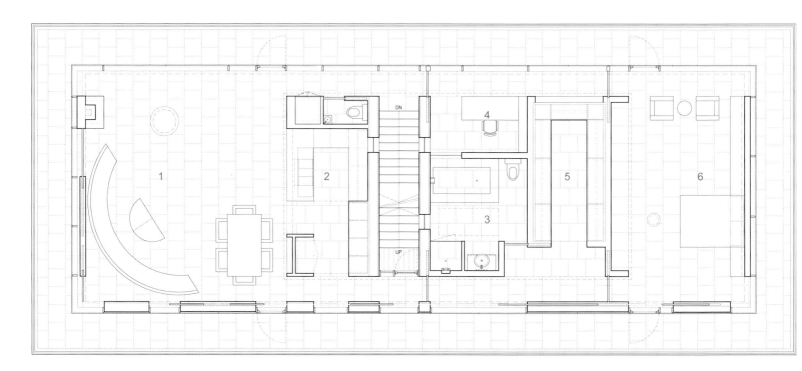

Master Plan

1. Living room
2. Kitchen
3. Bathroom
4. Library
5. Dress room
6. Master bedroom

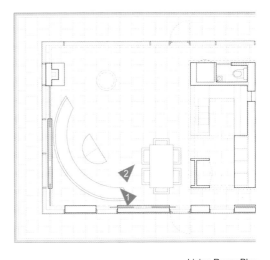

Living Room Plan

1. In the living room, there are same-sized windows at the top and bottom to provide a wormhole-like feeling to the parallel structure. The lighting effect of the top surface has balanced the openness of the top

2. "Visual relationship" means the relationship in which a person can look at an object but he/she cannot reach that. When a person looks at the ground across the river that has no bridge, and he/she communicates with that place through a window from a place without door, it is the visual relationship. The light of the lighttrough has defined the kitchen space

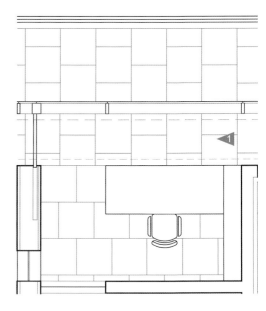

Library Plan

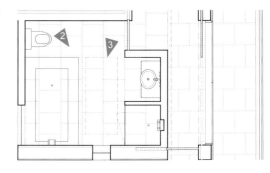

1. The study room and the kitchen were divided by a staircase but connected through a small window. The light and shadow effect of the linear top enhances the fluidity of the space

2. Person can look at the river through the study room while he/she is taking a shower or bath

3. The bathroom was connected to the sky through the window at the top and to the staircase that leads to the roof at the third floor through the window

Bathroom Plan

Architecture is to establish relationship. There are three kinds of relationships: physical relationship, visual relationship, and psychological relationship. The light and shadow effect of the top has enhanced the relationship

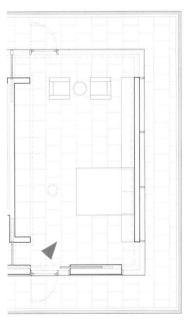

Master Bedroom Plan

52   The coordination of colours in the space

In home interior space design, the top design can play an important role in forming the colour harmony of the whole space. As the ultimate restrictive element, the surface design decides the volume of the space. Designed in colours with low colour saturation and high brightness, the ceiling can only be used as a setting to coordinate the relationship between different colours in contrast with the home furnishings with high colour saturation.

In this case, the designer creates an interior space in the classicist style by the use of some antiques, hand-made furniture and oil paintings matched up with other modern decorative elements which highlight the classicism aroma. A large amount of decorative moldings whose external texture can integrate into the modern decorative style are used in the ceiling design. The colours of the ceiling and the home furnishings keep in harmony with each other.

Project name: Town Classic **Completion date:** 2008 **Location:** Athens, Greece **Designer:** Cadena Design Group **Photographer:** Vangelis Rokkas **Area:** 325 sqm

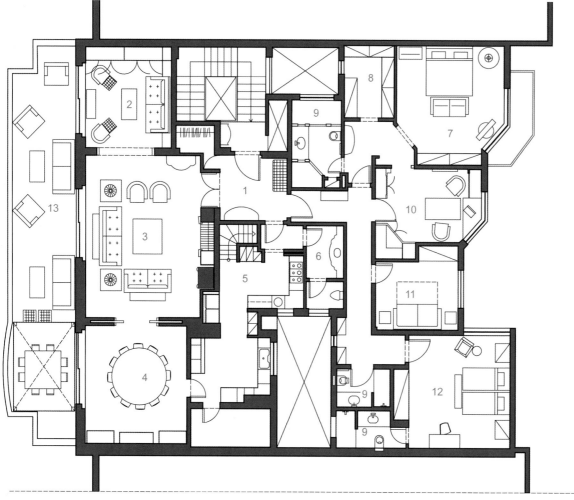

1. Entrance
2. TV room
3. Living room
4. Dining room
5. Kitchen
6. W.C.
7. Master bedroom
8. Walk-in
9. Bathroom
10. Study
11. Guestroom
12. Bedroom
13. Terrace

Master Plan

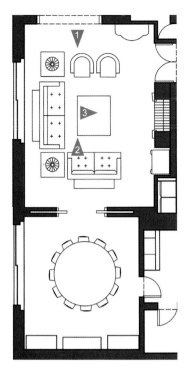

Living Room+Dining Room Plan

1. The architrave shape of the ceiling with classical decorative elements together with the modern aesthetic surface textures has created an elegant and colourful atmosphere

2. A revival of classical atmosphere is achieved by combining antique furniture with other contemporary items. The furniture was purchased along the years in antique shops and some of them were customised

3. The couple of the owners have a great preference for works of art and paintings and this is something that characterises their house. The walls are decorated with unique paintings of Greek and foreign artists

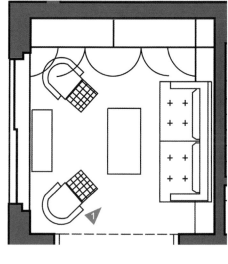

TV Room Plan

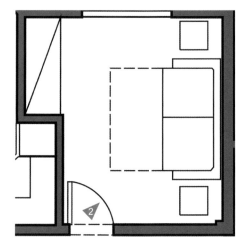

Guest Room Plan

1. Accurate lighting plays a very important role in this scenario. The house is easy-going and inviting every hour of the day, just by dimming the different light sources and giving emphasis to warm corners, items and painting
2. In the guestroom, a cosy and intimate atmosphere was created by using warm colours

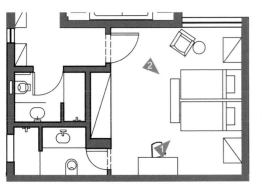

Bedroom+Bathroom Plan

1. The reflections of the ceiling in the master bedroom enhance the colour influence of the soft furnishings on the overall atmosphere

2. Materials with different textures have been used, such as wood, silk and wool, to give a feeling of luxury and timeless elegance in combination with latest technology lights that give the house a contemporary look

3. The master bathroom is decorated with Carrara marble in grey and white tones

53 New way of the experience

In home interior space design, the top surface with the task of defining the volume of the interior space needs to keep in harmony with the other surfaces, whether in colour or shape, so as to create the spatial tone jointly. Sometimes, the exaggerated ceiling design may break this harmonious relationship by reversing the volume of the space and breaking away from the whole space to become the decorative element, presenting people a new visual experience.

In this case, the designer adopts the pattern design in large area on the ceiling to increase the visual tension of the interior space.

Project name: Less Than A Tower **Completion date:** 2009 **Location:** Barcelona Spain **Designer:** Archikubik - Marc Chalamanch, Miquel Lacasta, Carmen Santana **Photographer:** Archikubik, Rene Lozano, José Hevia

1. The dark ceiling goes harmoniously with the size of the top of the dining area and relatively divides the overall space into different functional areas

2. The dark top goes harmoniously with the flexible divided living space, forming a comfortable relationship of the spatial composition

3. Interior apartment of east facade; the dark grey top has efficiently defined the functional areas of the living room, decorative and functional

1. The patterns that go through the ceiling have visually unified different functional areas, and the yellow-green island shelf against these patterns becomes the visual focus of the space

2. The colour palette of the ceiling goes harmoniously with the overall space, and the white base and the black patterns echo with the white wall and black window frames as well as the floor coverings

1/2. Top patterns in the warm colour inject the clean and simple space a sense of warmth, and yellow-green rug has enhanced this relationship naturally

54 The coordination of the space's composition 空间构图的协调

In this case, HEAD Architecture and Design has combined two apartments into one single apartment with tight budget and limited time. The apartment located in Hong Kong becomes a new living space with some oriental design in some corner. This residence provides all spaces for the family members' necessities, such as bathing, playing, eating and sleeping. All rooms have their own unique design and are featured by beautiful furniture. The living room looks so wide and more comfortable with grass carpet. Then, some oriental lamps were hanged in some spaces. The traditional Japanese style is felt in the bedroom; the bed is just laid on the floor. Yet this apartment also has modern style which is seen in the open bathroom. Within a door, a round Mosaic column instead defines the boundary. The round glass wall above the round bathtub allows one to look back into the bedroom and straight thought the bedroom window that gives a mountain view. At the moment, the wall looks like blank canvas; maybe as the family grows, they will have some pictures or memorials that can fill it.

Project name: Matsuki Residence **Completion date:** 2007 **Location:** Hong Kong, China **Designer:** HEAD Architecture **Photographer:** Mark Panckhurst **Area:** 160 sqm

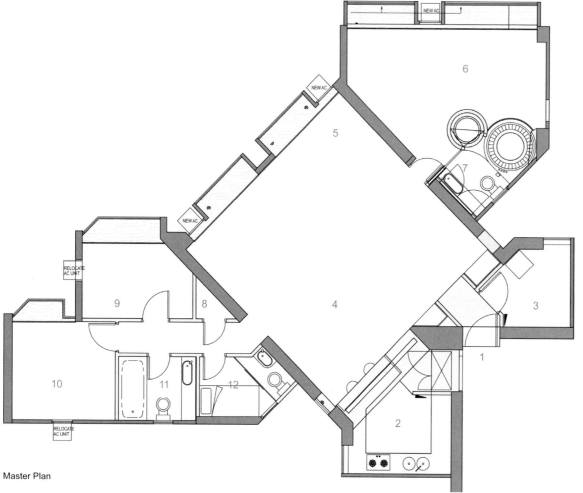

Master Plan

1. Entrance
2. Kitchen
3. Utility room
4. Dining
5. Living area
6. Master bedroom
7. Mater Bathroom
8. Store
9. Bedroom
10. Study
11. Bathroom
12. Maid

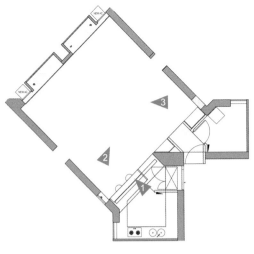

Living Area+Kitchen+Dining Plan

1. There are very few apartments that are contemporary and sophisticated. The Matsuki Residence is a fine example of the definition. The structure houses a single dramatic conceived space that has been created through the amalgamation of two apartments. An open plan coupled with series of flexible spaces has been incorporated for an informal flow and in order to accommodate changes that may erupt in future due to expansion of family. The interiors of the house are done in vibrant colourful shades that create an appealing aura

2. The walls may look a bit empty without decoration, but they are painted in different colours to make the house feel warmer

3. Since the whole space is opened up by two apartments, so the load-bearing beams become the main symbol of the space division. The linear windows together with the ceiling fan have highlighted the symmetry of the simple top structure, and thus naturally coordinated the relationship between the space's composition

55 The choice of wood

Wood, as the interior decorative material, enjoys incomparable advantages with the warm and gentle colour and the rough texture that induces people to touch it.

In this case, the designer adopts walnut, marble, stainless steel and steel frameworks in the public area of the living room and the kitchen to realise the client's desire of creating a workshop style space with a nostalgic touch. A livable interior environment with a strong industrial sense has been produced through the successful collocation of these materials.

Project name: Prospect House **Completion date:** 2010 **Location:** Seattle, Washington, USA **Designer:** Janof Hald Architecture **Photographer:** Benjamin Benschneider **Area:** 526 sqm
Award name: American Institute of Steel Construction 2011 National Certificate of Recognition

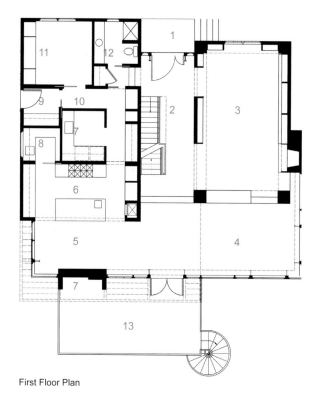

First Floor Plan

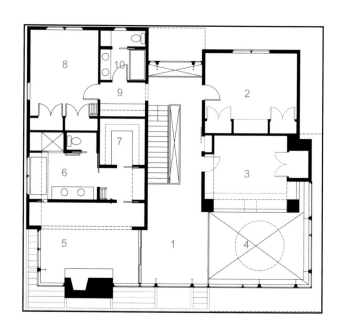

Second Floor Plan

1. Porch	8. Pantry
2. Entry	9. Vestibule
3. Living	10. Hall
4. Dining	11. Office
5. Breakfast	12. Powder room
6. Kitchen	13. Deck
7. Barbecue	

1. Lounge	7. Dressing
2. Bedroom	8. Bedroom
3. Study	9. Homework
4. Open to below	10. Bath
5. Master bedroom	
6. Master bath	

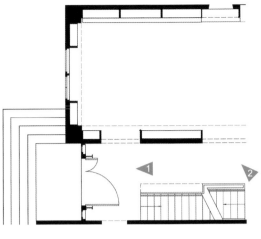

Entry+Living Plan

1. The bronze front door is by a local artisan; its assymetrical leaves can both be opened to welcome guests for the large events regularly hosted here. The entry hall links these two spaces to the open kitchen, which is finished in the same refined materials as the living room

2. The house is designed for entertaining and convivial family living. The main level contains a library-like living room that steps down to the dramatic two-storey dining room

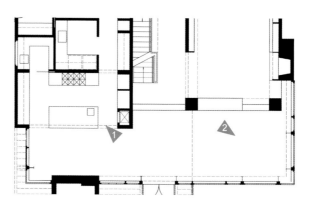

Kitchen+Dining Plan

1. Walnut cabinetry in the main living areas and kitchen is paired with creamy Calacatta marble and stainless steel

2. Because the owners wished to maintain a domestic yet industrially vintage look to their home, the house employs conventional wide-flange steel in a wind-braced frame, giving the architects an opportunity to use an unusual amount of glass in a two-storey-high, fifty-foot-wide wall. Combining a rigid steel frame with residential grade wood windows created the look of an old factory

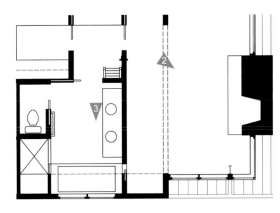

Master Bedroom+Master Bath Plan

1. On the second floor, the upstairs lounge, which sits outside the master suite

2. The materials used throughout the house were chosen for their timelessness and sensual qualities

3. The master bath is entirely sheathed in marble, and polished nickel fixtures and hardware gleam against its honed surface

56 The choice of stone

Stone, as the traditional building material, possesses the solid, practical and beautiful qualities. The decorative characteristic of the decorative stone is embodied by its colour, pattern, luster and texture.

In this case, the designer selects stone as the main decorative material of the fireplace and the like to highlight the volume and texture of the living room.

Project name: Stratford Mountain **Completion date:** 2008 **Location:** Austin, USA **Designer:** Dick Clark Architecture **Photographer:** Dick Clark Architecture **Area:** 677.24 sqm

1. The residence's internal spaces are simply organised with living space on the ground floor which is focus towards the north and the outdoor terrace. The size of all openings is exaggerated in dimension, giving the effect of a larger wall opening and providing a greater of transparency and openness throughout

2. The project included new cabinetry and appliances in the kitchen, new cabinetry and closet redesign

3. Bedroom spaces direct to the distant views to the east

57 The choice of metal

In home interior space design, the metal material is mainly used as the load-bearing structure and the decorative finishing. The main feature of the metal material is its shining lustre: the steel and the aluminium showcase the dynamic of the era; the copper seems more gorgeous and elegant; the iron looks simple, unsophisticated and dignified.

In this case, the designer selects the metal material as the decorative material of the terrace and the façade of the building to make a sharp contrast with the rough natural environment.

Project name: Blue Sky Home **Completion date:** 2009 **Location:** Yucca Valley, America **Designer:** O2 Architecture **Photographer:** Nuvue Interactive **Area:** 93 sqm

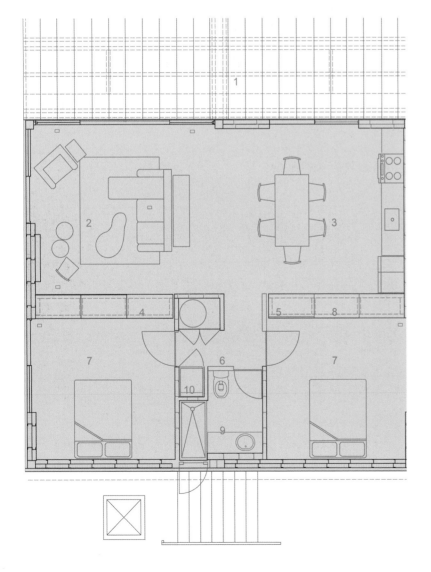

Master Plan

1. Balcony
2. Living room
3. Kitchen
4. Audio/visual
5. Pantry
6. Vesibule
7. Bedroom
8. Closet1
9. Bath room
10. Laundry

1. The decorative effect of the metal materials is highlighted by the raw wood

2. Seamless 30 square metres outdoor deck floats above the site on structurally efficient columns and beams of light gauge steel

1. Interiors are defined by the placement of storage cabinetry, eliminating interior framed walls. The metal full-height sliding door and the exposed balcony become the main interface to divide the indoor and outdoor space, and the natural materials and industrial quality play important roles in the decoration of the space

2. The homeowner asked for a modest size, open and adaptable floor plan that was sustainably conceived with durable materials

3. The metal texture contrasts with the raw wood sharply

4. The design would serve as a prototype for a future line of prefabricated "system-built" homes. Emphasis was given to flexible site placement; and ensuring minimal environmental impact while maximising view potential and required privacy

5. The bathroom module, containing all home mechanical, plumbing, and electrical services, is built off-site and delivered with the flat packed "system-of-components"

58 The choice of the plain concrete

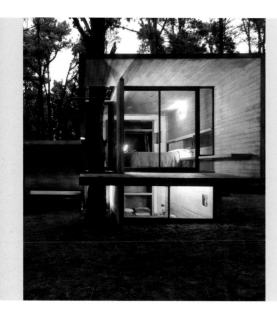

Different from the ordinary concrete, the plain concrete looks natural and solemn with smooth surface, clear edges and corners, which are formed only by painting the transparent protective agent on its surface but without any decoration. This architectural style uses the naked grey concrete material as the fundamental key decorated with the texture left by removing the formwork and the simple spatial form to construct the Zen-style interior space.

In this case, the designer selects the plain concrete, the glass and the steel as the main building and decorative materials, creating a simple space while integrating the exterior landscape.

Project name: JD House **Completion date:** 2009 **Location:** Buenos Aires, Argentina **Designer:** BAKarquitectos **Photographer:** Gustavo Sosa Pinilla **Area:** 149 sqm

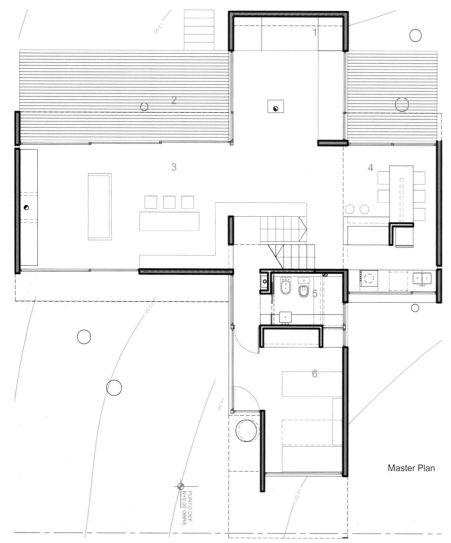

Master Plan

1. Entry
2. Balcony
3. Living room
4. Kitchen
5. Bathroom
6. Living room

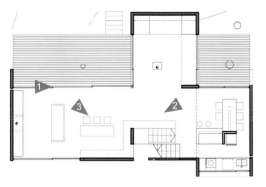

Living Room Plan

1. Briefly, an outer skin made only by two materials - concrete and glass - resolves the integration with the landscape and the formal, structural and functional issues apart from the facades and the maintenance

2. The volumes are crossed perpendicularly and in mid levels

3. The central place of the house, the living room is an L-shaped space, and an outdoor terrace is located on either side of it. It makes a spacious, rectangular space together with the adjoining kitchen and dining area. The boundaries between the interior space and the terraces are configured entirely with full-height glass doors, offering a sense of great openness to the space when the doors are open

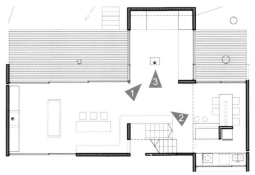

Living Room Plan

1. The social area had to be large enough with the possibility of being adapted to different uses as they frequently receive many friends. The kitchen had to be integrated to the social area and finally it was especially specified that they wanted generous outdoor expansions

2. Designers conceived the house like two pure prisms, placed in a clearing among the trees

3. The project gives a comfortable presence even though it stands in rugged terrain

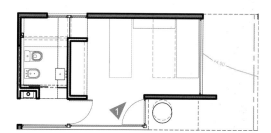

1. The strong slope of the land was exploited to hide part of the programme, reducing in this way the presence of the built volume. With this volumetric arrangement designers endowed the house with all the required places without loosing an independent use of each one. The principal bedroom has its own terrace under roof

2. The facade decoration made up with glass and mirror under the effects of transparence and reflection enhances the texture of concrete

Bedroom Plan

59 The choice of ceramic

The ceramic is a frequently used decoration material at present. Ceramic usually stands for the general term for potteries and porcelains. The potteries with some extent of water absorption and the rough surface may produce a guff and hoarse voice after being knocked; the porcelains enjoys higher sintering degree than potteries with enamel layers but without the ability of water absorption.

In this case, the designer selects the vitreous china to make the limited interior space simpler and wider through strong ground reflection.

Project name: The Canary **Completion date:** 2007 **Location:** Singapore City, Singapore **Designer:** Ong&Ong Pte Ltd **Photographer:** Ong&Ong Pte Ltd **Area:** 266 sqm

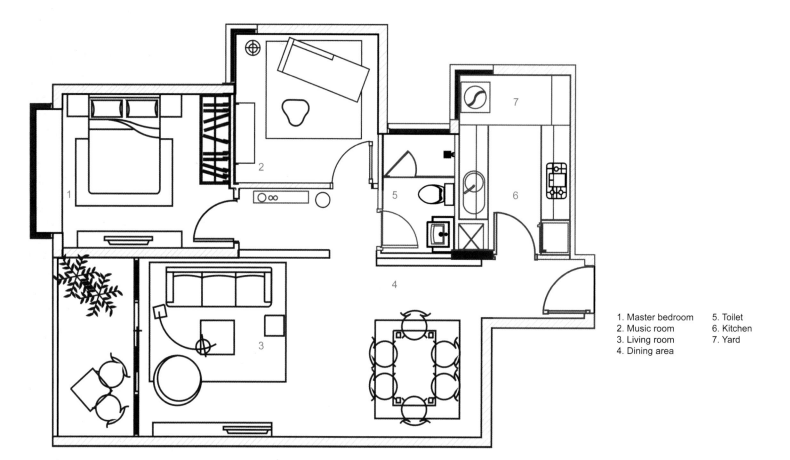

1. Master bedroom
2. Music room
3. Living room
4. Dining area
5. Toilet
6. Kitchen
7. Yard

Master Plan

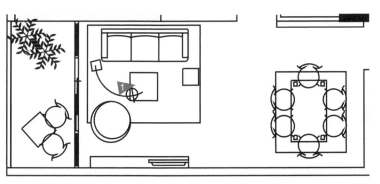

Living Room+Dining Area Plan

1. The reflective ceramic floor together with the simple shape of the space has created a modern aesthetic pop art style

2. A functional white high gloss kitchen with minimal equipment is installed. The texture of the ceramic injects this area a sense of simplicity

In the study room, the matte floor together with the warm lightings from the background has created a quiet atmosphere, and the dark grey carpet has defined the reading area

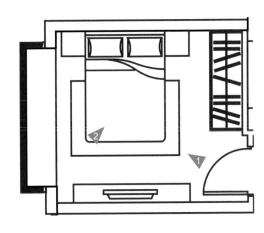

Master Bedroom Plan

1. White and bright colours were selected for the 2-bedroom flat. Graphic motifs were hand painted on the wall - this is unique craftwork that still could be found in Vietnam

2. The bedroom was designed with darker hues. Typically, in the Vietnamese culture, darker tones are perceived as luxury

3. Toilet tiles selected in grey hues exudes a fresh modern ambience

60 The choice of glass

In home interior space design, glass has been gradually developed to regulate light and heat, save energy and protect the environment, control noise, reduce structural weight and improve the environment. The glass after being coloured and polished has increasingly become the significant decorative element of the interior space.

In this case, the designer makes the space wider and creates a tough spatial ambience by the use of the glass material.

Project name: Camargo Correa Brooklin **Completion date:** 2010 **Location:** São Paulo, Brazil **Designer:** Fernanda Marques Arquitetos Associados **Photographer:** Demian Golovaty **Area:** 74 s

Master Plan

1. Kitchen
2. Living room
3. Dining room
4. Balcony
5. Master suite

1. The main goal, according to the design, is to create an opening area and make the apartment looking like a loft

2. The design is to eliminate as many walls as possible, in order to get spaces as integrated as possible

3. In the case, the client is looking for solutions that can give the visitors the sensation of being penetrating a "masculine", modern and current home, and this idea is crucial to determine the furniture and the finishing materials

4. Lighting is enhanced with lowered ceilings and recessed lighting details, and in this way it is able to produce multiple effects

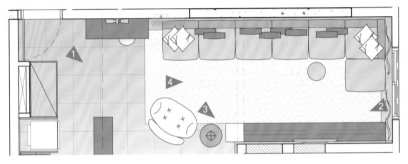

Living Room Plan

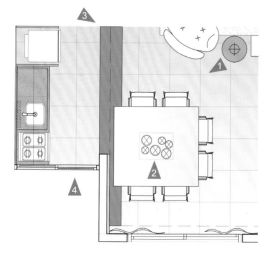

Kitchen+Dining Room Plan

1. The kitchen, for instance, is completely opened up to the living room and the dining room

2. The design believes that open space can make a small apartment feel spacious; make it look big, generous in terms of circulation

3. The kitchen ensures enlarged spaces, as well as full integration of all the social areas

4. The white mirror at the entrance extends the overall space greatly

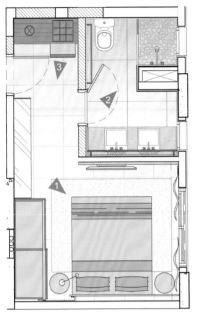

Bedroom Plan

1. By privacy reasons, the master bedroom just remains the only completely isolated place in the home

2. The white glass partition of the bathroom has effectively expanded the space visually

3. The spacious and transparent storage space reflects the owner's personality of confidence and calmness

61　The choice of textile

The fabric furnishings in the home interior space enjoy the rich colour and lustre and the soft texture. Different kinds of fabrics collocate with each other in accordance with the practicality, comfortableness and artistic quality of the interior function.

In this case, the designer successfully creates the decorative style of the French Classicism by the collocation and combination of different fabrics in line with the client's desire.

Project name: Paris Apartment **Completion date:** 2006 **Location:** Paris, France **Designer:** Alberto Pinto **Photographer:** Jacques Pépion **Area:** 500 sqm

1. The client's desire was to recapture something of the refinement of the French Grand Siecle, into which was integrated a prestigious array of contemporary artworks. This commission allowed the designer to display the characteristic flavour of his work

2. Designer's creativity allows him to break free of the doctrinal straitjacket of the classical, letting a taste for things past inform the present and add to the pleasure of each passing day

3. Soft furnishings cheer up the window surroundings, while couches and armchairs are covered and trimmed with precious fabrics

4. Art and authenticity are equally instrumental in its restoration: the stone, the marquetry flooring, the woodwork, the painted dados, woodwork, and doors, and the delicacy of the carving by classical ornamentistes all conspire in a backdrop that sets off the grace of the bijou furniture found on the antique market or else recreated to the scale of the rooms and following the rules of the style

1. To situate the daring art collection within a typically eighteenth-century framework thus became an aesthetic challenge, rather like those blockbuster exhibitions in which avant-garde works are hung in a period setting

2. The contemporary and the classical enhance each other in an oxymoron typical of Paris, a city where bustling creative energy has always had to vie with the magnificence of the past

1. Lying at the heart of this classical composition, the contemporary art brings with it surprise and buoyancy

2. Each juxtaposition participates in the unmistakable, highly individual world to which designer is so attached

62 The change of pattern and background

"Pattern" and "background" stand for the flooring, the furniture on it and the interactive relations between the two sides. The changes of the pattern and the background mean to exert an influence on human behaviour and psychology through this interactive relation. In home interior space design, both the flooring and the furniture possess some function of space limitation. Once the space is limited, it is endowed with the ability of defining the life style. Therefore, the division of the plane functions of the interior space is the process of coordinating the relations between the pattern and the background.

In this case, the designer re-establishes the division of the plane functions by transforming the original space and forms an orderly space sequence through the reasonable arrangement of the modular furniture.

Project name: House Leuven with Pool **Completion date:** 2009 **Location:** Leuven, Belgium **Designer:** Montagna Lunga **Photographer:** Marc Sourbron **Area:** 290 sqm

1. The texture of the flooring has continued the tactile experience of the wood veneer wall, and contrasts with the cold partition wall sharply. Abstract carving together with the wood wall finishes and stainless steel as well as floor covering forms a rich relationship of the spatial composition

2. The designer renovated the interior completely. It took more than a year to complete the renovation

3. Everything was custom made. It was a heavy renovation in terms of difficulty and logistics

4. The transition of the flooring implies the conversion of the space environment, and the calm living room and smart kitchen have been appropriately expressed by the changes of the flooring

63 The alternation of the volume

The wall undertakes the task of the division of the home interior space. Such space division methods as the load bearing wall, the nonbearing wall, the light partition wall and the partition wall divide the homogenised interior space into the space regions with different space volumes. A complete and orderly space sequence is formed through the combination of these space regions.

In this case, the designer divides the enclosed building plane into lots of flowing spaces by the use of a group of partition walls so as to provide multiple possibilities for people's activities.

Project name: Twin Houses **Completion date:** 2008 **Location:** Bogotá, Colombia **Designer:** MGP Arquitecturay Urbanismo **Photographer:** Andrés Valbuena, Jorge Gamboa, Rodrigo Dávila **Area:** 1,136 sqm **Award:** Asocreto, Concrete Excellence Prizes, September 2010

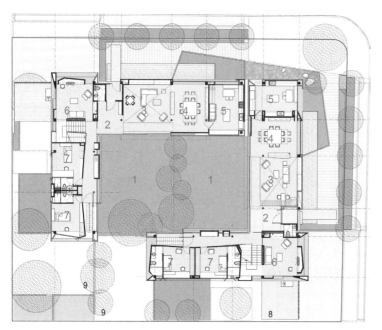

First Floor Plan

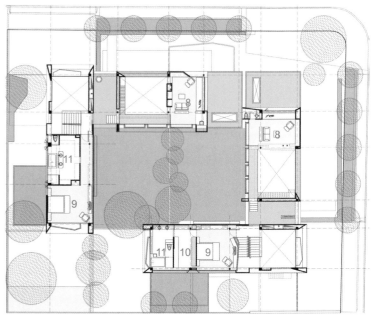

Second Floor Plan

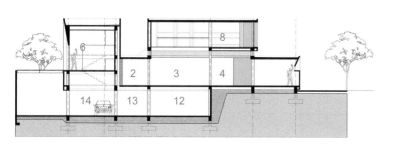

Section Plan

1. Central patio	8. Studio
2. Main entrance	9. Main bedroom
3. Living room	10. Walking closet
4. Dining room	11. Bathroom
5. Kitchen	12. Electrical plant
6. Family room	13. Laundry room
7. Bedroom	14. Parking

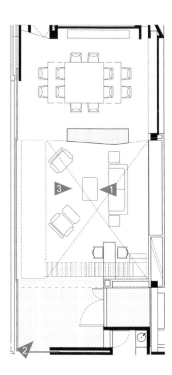

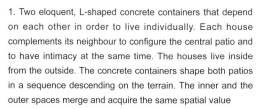
Living Room Plan

1. Two eloquent, L-shaped concrete containers that depend on each other in order to live individually. Each house complements its neighbour to configure the central patio and to have intimacy at the same time. The houses live inside from the outside. The concrete containers shape both patios in a sequence descending on the terrain. The inner and the outer spaces merge and acquire the same spatial value

2. From the outside, the exposed wood's texture complements the concrete's hardness

3. The project is the result of the dream of two families: the architect's family and his sister's family. Each one composed by four members, father, mother and two children. The houses were designed for the families to grow independently or together. The architect designed two family houses very much alike. A pair of twin houses in a very special place in a city with a privileged weather, where the light changes the colour of vegetation every hour

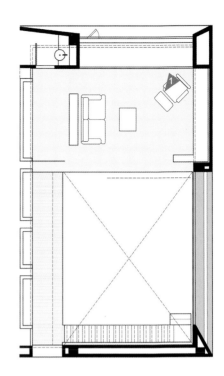

Studio Plan

1. The owner's studio is developed as a floating box, located on the second floor in the last bent container, with the purpose of isolating this space

3. The concrete shells enclose the interior divisions, all being dry walls or wood walls. This way, with the passing of time, the interior distribution is changeable according to each family

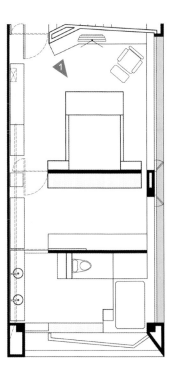

Bedroom+Bathroom Plan

1. The houses are like luggage, hard on the outside and soft in the inside in order to let the changes in the family transform the interior spaces

2. The concrete walls bend and fold to show the plasticity of the material and to reinforce the entrance of light against the concrete

64 The definition of pleasure

In home interior space design, the ceiling design brings about the visual experience that represents the materialisation and extention of the territoriality of individual space. This kind of spatial integrity is people's inherent psychological need. Any visual changes on the basis of the integrity will produce the delighted experience effects.

In this case, the designer intensifies the dynamic effects of the interior space by combining the natural lighting and the artificial lighting. Above all, the lighting effect on the ceiling of the living room will change with time.

Project name: Sinu River House **Completion date:** 2010 **Location:** Monteria, Colombia **Designer:** Antonio Sofan **Photographer:** Carlos Tobon **Area:** 500 sqm

Master Plan

1. Living	6. Maid's room	11. Bedroom
2. Dining	7. Bedroom	12. Master bedroom
3. Kitchen	8. Bathroom	13. Master bath
4. Garage	9. Walk-in closet	14. Pool
5. Laundry	10. Studio	

Entrance+Pool Plan

1. The entrance vestibule divides the bedrooms quarter from the living spaces. It is open on both sides to allow the breeze blowing from the river to go through the house after it is freshened by the water in the pool
2. The pool

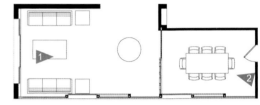

Living+Dining Plan

1. Baby blue shear drapes were selected to achieve an optical illusion of coolness under the overhang. Also, the blue tinted glass and matching ceiling colour help complete the breezed effect of the shaded environment. The living and dining rooms have soaring ceilings which reach 5 metres. Patterned painted cement tiles in shades of blue were used to clad a coffer above the living room ceiling which is as well emphasised by a light cove

2. Even though the space flows seamlessly between the living and dining, both rooms are separated by a white lacquered wood door that forms a plaid pattern when open. A much more subtle geometry is used to highlight the ceiling above the dining room, a pattern formed by bare fluorescent light bulbs flush to the face of the drywall ceiling

3. High ceilings also soar in the kitchen. They help exhaust the hot air through the high clerestories

1. The guest's bedroom faces east and overlooks into a landscaped access courtyard

2. The ample master bedroom faces the infinity pool and the river beyond. The integration with nature reassures that this house is a breathtaking example of habitable contemporary architecture

3. Master bath

Master Bedroom+Master Bath Plan

65 Space magician

Home interior space design is a technology, but also visual arts that all its design techniques about shape, colour and texture focus on creating the meaningful ambience. With the development of the times, the concept of modelling has always represented the radical concept revolution which will follow the developing trend from complex to simple. During this process, the visualisation of material will gradually liberate itself from the simple modelling as the independent decorative vocabulary and express the spatial quality.

In this case, the designer uses the ordinary materials to create a comfortable living environment. The collocation and combination of the materials express the designer's understanding of life quality, among which the sustainable design concept is also one of the important design methods.

Project name: The Hillside House **Completion date:** 2010 **Location:** California, USA **Designer:** SB Architects **Photographer:** Mariko Reed/Matthew Millman/Robert Bengtson **Area:** 197 sqm

First Floor Plan

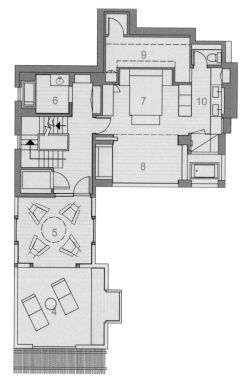

Second Floor Plan

Third Floor Plan

1. Guest bedroom
2. Entry porch
3. Laundry
4. Terrace
5. Yoga deck
6. Baby
7. Master bedroom
8. Master terrace
9. Dressing
10. Master bath
11. Office
12. Outdoor kitchen & family
13. Upper terrace
14. Living
15. Dining
16. Kitchen

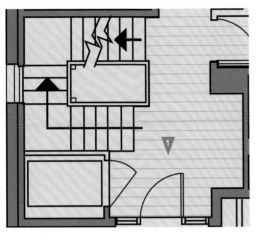

Entry Porch Plan

1. Front door detail
2. The design of the staircase's lightings
3. Upper floor landing

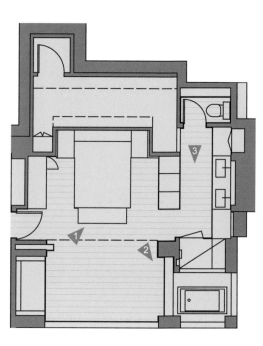

Master Bedroom+Master Bath+Dressing+Master Terrace Plan

1. The four-storey home steps back into the hillside, working its way around the trees, driven by the views, and defined by the intimate relationship between indoors and outdoors

2. Private and living zones are set on their own floors; every space has its own private terrace, and every window embraces views of the surrounding trees or the San Francisco skyline in the distance

3. Design elements crafted locally from reclaimed materials – such as hand-crafted tile from Sausalito-based Heath Ceramics and steelwork from artisan Brian Kennedy – give this project deep roots in the community, making it sustainable from a community standpoint

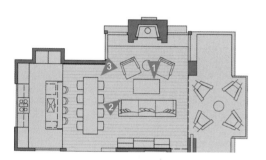

Kitchen+Dining+Living+Upper Terrance Plan

1. Most of the sustainable solutions were carefully planned, but some came about simply through the synergies created by bringing all of these innovative designers, suppliers and artisans together with a singular mission

2. A covered terrace acts as an indoor/outdoor family room off the main living level, visually and psychologically expanding the space

3. Every inch of this LEED Platinum custom home has been designed to maximise its sustainability, in direct response to the site, trees and views. Consequently, this home lives far larger than its actual footprint, but with an impact that is far less

4. View of indoor, outdoor room & living room beyond

DECORATIVE DESIGN PRINCIPLES

66 Unity and contrast

Working with the spacial qualities of the architecture, the interior design has become a science in itself. The elements used in artistic expression of any visual art such as shape, colour, and texture are also used in modelling an architectural form. Through this modelling with the selection and placement of interior furnishings, the designer must create an environment with a deeper connection to the owner living within. Over time, the designers' design aesthetic has developed from the complex to the simple, radically changing the way they conceptualise space and utilise decorative elements.

In this case, the designer uses ordinary materials to create a comfortable living environment. The collocation and combination of materials express the designer's understanding of life quality, among which the sustainable design concept is one of the important instruments.

Project name: Winter Oceanfront Residence **Completion date:** 2007 **Location:** Hillsboro Beach, Florida, USA **Interior Designer:** Kathryn Scott Design Studio Ltd **Architect:** Max Wolfe Sturman Architects **Photographer:** Daniel Newcomb **Area:** 1, 021 sqm

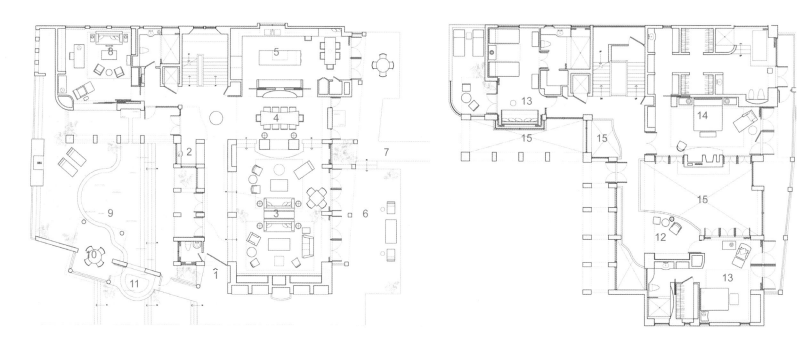

First Floor Plan

Second Floor Plan

1. Entrance	6. Front deck	11. Jacuzzi
2. Bar	7. Wood deck to ocean	12. Library
3. Living room	8. Guest bedroom/office	13. Guest bedroom
4. Dining room	9. Pool	14. Master bedroom
5. Kitchen	10. Gazebo	15. Open to hallway below

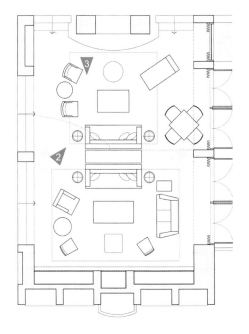

Living Room Plan

1. Mexican Saultillo floor tiles were selected for their handmade quality, with the ones showing animal footprints (created when dogs walked over the wet terracotta while they were being made) left for the most predominant areas, so they would not be missed

2. In building the house, no corner beads were used in the plaster wall construction, allowing the surfaces and contours to be delightfully irregular

3. The custom doors and cabinetry were all made from Cypress wood, which has a rustic character often used by Addison Mizner, famous for his Spanish Colonial Revival architecture of old South Florida. The wall colours were not created by normal house paint but with natural powdered pigments incorporated in the wet wall plaster

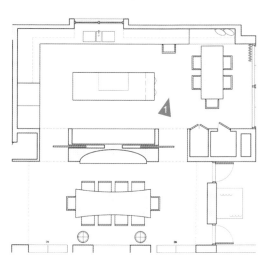

Kitchen+Dining Room Plan

2. The Mexican architect, Luis Barragan, was the inspiration in selecting the colours of the house and the way they were applied

3. The library

1. The client wanted comfort and high quality furnishings cohesive with the casual serenity of the architecture itself

2. The exterior doors and windows were made of mahogany for their visual warmth and rich character. The custom designed bronze interior and exterior railings have developed a rich patina, and ages gracefully. The material was selected because of how it withstands the harsh sun and salt air

3. The large wood trusses and wood plank ceilings were hand coloured to show slight variations of faded browns. The house is luxurious without being pretentious; a wonderful place to slow down to enjoy the simple pleasures of life

67 Principal and subordinate & emphasis

Home furnishings is far from piling up them blindly but forming a harmonious relationship through proper organisation and coordination, during which the relation between the principal and the subordinate is a key element. The quality of the interior space can be expressed in the most directive and effective way by the display of the principal furnishings.

In this case, the designer chooses a set of modular couch to divide the space and the decorative artworks in Southeast Asian style to match it. The collocation in the principal and subordinate mode, simple and visualised, not only meets the functional requirements but creates the interior spatial ambience.

Project name: Dahua - Island Against Water **Completion date:** 2008 **Location:** Chengdu, China **Designer:** Hong Kong Fong Hong Architects **Photographer:** Wang Jianlin **Area:** 178.9 sqm
Main materials: floors, stone, mosaic, silver mirror, paint

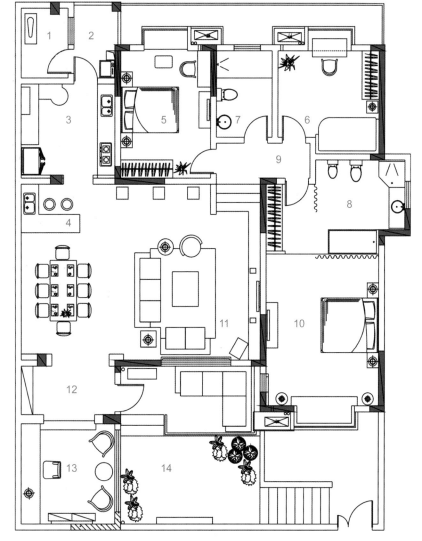

Master Plan

1. Multi-function room
2. Balcony
3. Chinese kitchen
4. Western food island
5. Elderly room
6. Children's room
7. Guest bathroom
8. Master bathroom
9. Foyer
10. Master bedroom
11. Living room
12. Hall
13. Study
14. Garden

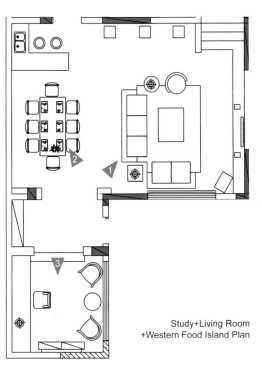

Study+Living Room
+Western Food Island Plan

1. Designers have built it into the Southeast Asian-style casual house. Dark wood, sectional floor, dark mosaic, art furniture and many ornaments all give full expression of the Southeast Asia's living style. It is an ideal quiet haven for the busy owner to relax and enjoy life

2. The integration of the living room and dining room greatly expands the hall. The West-food table at the corner of the dining room can also be used as bar

68 Balance and stability

The decorative design of the home interior space is comprised of the interface of the architectural decoration and the furnishings. The design process becomes a coordination of various kinds of decorative vocabulary with the abstract concept of spatial composition to create equilibrium and stability. The interaction of shape, pattern, scale and proportion defines the style and decorative elements included in the interior.

In this case, the furnishings are mixed together with the art, and at times the furniture becomes the art through a conceptual installation within the interior space, thus forming a curious relationship between the practical and conceptual. In addition the architecture itself becomes an art defined not only by its sculptural and spatial qualities, but by the way, it directs light to pass through the rooms throughout the day.

Project name: Upstate New York Residence **Completion date:** 2007 **Location:** Ancram, New York, USA **Interior Designer:** Kathryn Scott Design Studio Ltd **Architect:** HHF Architects GmbH + Ai Weiwei **Photographer:** Ellen McDermott **Area:** 483 sqm

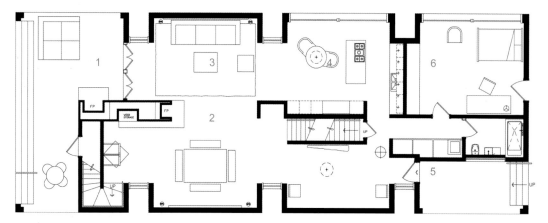

First Foor Plan

1. Covered terrace
2. Dining
3. Living
4. Kitchen
5. Entrance
6. Atelier

Second Floor Plan

1. Library
2. Guest bathroom
3. Guest bedroom
4. Guest closet
5. Master closet
6. Master bathroom
7. Master bedroom

1. The structure is diminished to the essence of utmost simplicity, not needing or wanting anything more. The furnishings are also art forms in themselves, adding to the cultural quality of the house

2. The architects had a significant art collection to consider when designing the building form and window placement

3. Some windows are placed high, above one's head, to sculpt the sunlight during its daily path, and others are slivers of openings, with carefully placed expanses to open the room to view of the nature outside

4. The chairs, tables and sofas had to be comfortable without disrupting the harmony of the interior architecture. The desire was to use just enough furniture to serve that uprose and no more

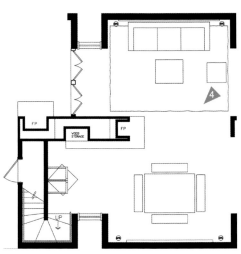

Living+Dining Plan

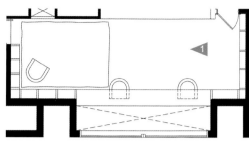

1. Patterns, textures and materials were all controlled very carefully so the perfect balance would be achieved between the furnishings, the architecture, the art and the light

2. Furnishings were selected and placed in the rooms as part of the overall composition

3. The furnishings were selected for their compatibility to the owner's aesthetics, as well as their comfort and livability

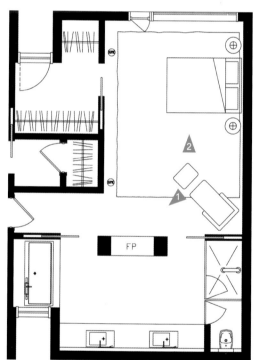

Master Bedroom+Master Bathroom Plan

1. Although art takes many forms within the house, the comfort of the owners living among it remained a priority

2. The interior is intended to be experienced within itself, but the occasional placement of a large expanse of windows makes the view of the landscape appear as if it were a living work of art on the wall

3. The interior furnishings and colours remain quiet so as not to compete or distract one's attention away from the art, and harmonious with the changing light patterns as they dance across the rooms

69 Contrast and delicate difference

Contrast and difference in decorative design are the redefinition of homogenised space. In the interior space with a unified style, the differential of decorative design represents the spatial quality. The subtle differences are demonstrated through the shape, colour and texture of the decorative elements. A tranquil living environment where you can meditate peacefully can be created by the contrast and difference of the decorative elements.

In this case, the designer designs a free space belonging to the client herself, an office lady, in accordance with her work's features. The natural and casual interior spatial ambience is presented through the texture changes of the red brick wall.

Project name: Changhong Gong Di **Completion date:** 2010 **Location:** Taipei, China **Designer:** Huang Penglin (Janus Huang) / Taiper Base Design Center **Photographer:** Wang Jishou (Black) **Area:** 140 sqm

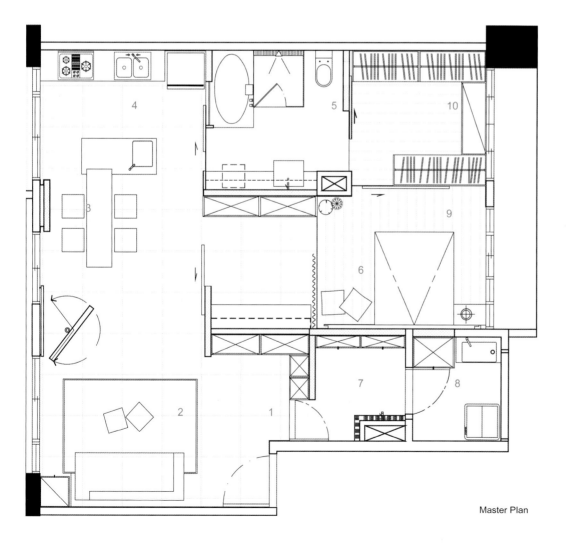

Master Plan

1. Foyer
2. Living area
3. Dining area/bar
4. Kitchen
5. Masters bathroom
6. Reading area
7. Doggie area
8. Laundry/storage
9. Masters bedroom
10. Walk-in closet

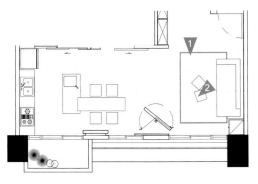

Living Area+Dining Area/Bar+Kitchen Plan

1. The original large windows have been retalined to lead more natural light into the interior space and open the dark middle part

2. Since the public area is full of light, so the designer removes the kitchen space that ever stood in a corner next to the French window in the public area. The dining table has extended the desktop, and integrated all of the equipment, facilitating the hostess who prefers to the light dishes to clean up. In addition, in order to create a spacious public area as much as possible and meet the owner's need, the designer has chosen the moveable and rotatable way to place the television onto the wall next to the living room and dining room. The place of television can be adjusted according to the use, so as to enhance the varying function of the fixed arrangement

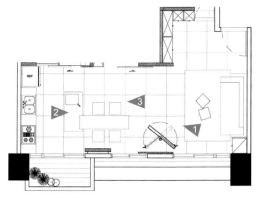

Living Area+Dining Area/Bar+Kitchen Plan

1. This house is designed for a single woman who shuttles between Hong Kong and Taiwan, even though she could spend little time at home, she still needs a free space to relax herself

2. To find a favourite style of the space needs to develop from the various forms in mind

3. The square internal structure is divided into public area and private area. The red brick main walls painted with white colour together with the uneven brick texture inject the room a sense of natural leisure

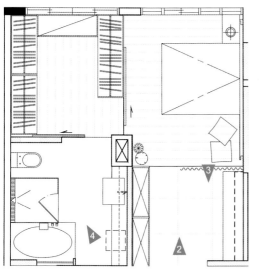

Reading Area+Master Bedroom+Master Bathroom Plan

1. The revolving generatrix of the bedroom conncets the dressing room and bathroom together

2. Since the owner is single, less storage cabinets are placed. According to the different using requirements and scale, the designer has arragned the storage area carefully. He believes that there is a close relationship between the storage function and the user, so the design not only needs to meet the immediate requirements but also should take the future change into account

3. In the bedroom, the work area has integrated with the large bookcases seamlessly, and the sliding door could enclose an independent private space

70 Rhythm and tune

The building has always been compared to music flows and the interior space is just like the romantic tunes. Different elements such as structures, materials and furnishings can be organised together in a specific rhythm and cadence to form the consecutive and luxuriant visual experience. This kind of rhythm and cadence can be presented by the alternation of different functional areas and the visual tension demonstrated by the decorative design.

In this case, the designer marks off different spatial environments in order according to the spatial form of the public and the private space, creating the interior spatial ambience with a strong sense of rhythm. Meanwhile, the rhythm has been intensified by allocating different furnishings to various rooms.

Project name: Greenwich Village Bachelor Residence **Completion date:** 2009 **Location:** New York, USA **Designer:** JansonGoldStein llp **Photographer:** Mikiko Kikuyama **Area:** 186 sqm

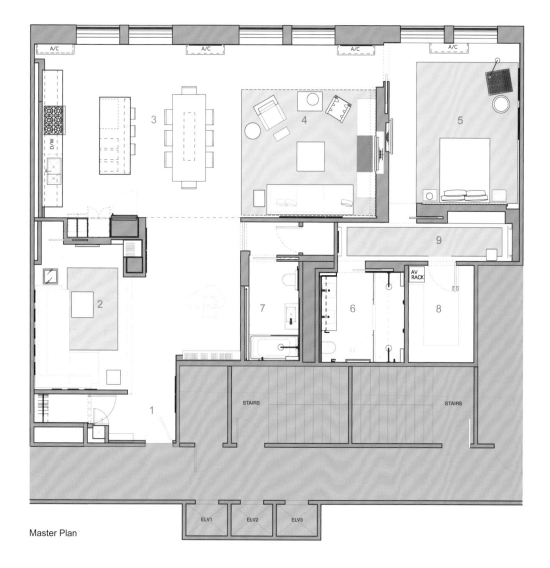

Master Plan

1. Entrance
2. Kitchen
3. Dining hall
4. Living room
5. Bedroom
6. Washroom
7. Bathroom
8. AV rack
9. Corridor

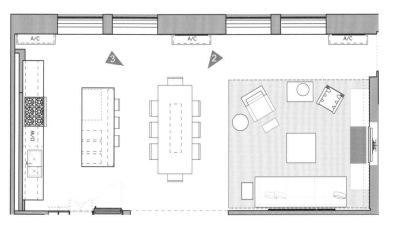

1. The living area features multiple patterns and textures, and an eclectic collection of furniture and art pieces

2. There is a silk rug in warm tones with a herring bone pattern and a custom designed sofa in crushed velvet

3. The plan is open and the spaces flow together with little separation between functions. The main room features the kitchen, dining and living areas. The LCD screen is set into the wall of charcoal coloured plaster with European walnut panels above. A custom designed lacquer piece houses the video equipment and provides a surface for photographs and objects

Kitchen+Dining Hall+Living Room Plan

1. The island provides additional cooking and storage capabilities and of course a place to gather around. It is wrapped in French marble and its face is constructed of mirrored polish stainless, placed on an angle, so it reflects the fumed oak floor as well as the clear acrylic stools. The materials were chosen for their warmth, richness and classic feel

2. The kitchen is composed of European walnut and stainless steel, a portion of which (refrigerator, espresso, wine) is recessed and integrated into the wall. The remaining programme of the kitchen is built as furniture and floating objects

3. Connecting the dressing area and bathroom is a hall with a patterned wall covered by a pink patterned runner which leads into the bathroom

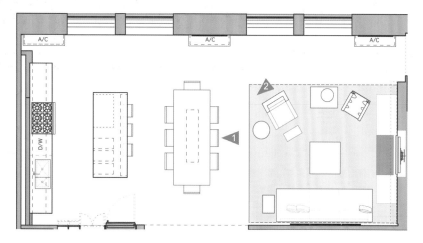

Kitchen+Dining Hall+Living Room Plan

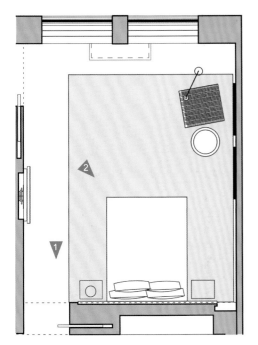

Bedroom Plan

1/2. The soothing celadon silk carpet was chosen along with a leather eel skin headboard in chocolate brown. A vintage mid-century floor lamp, a chair by Jean Nouvel, and ottomans by Milo Baumann compose the seating area in the bedroom

3/4. A double showerhead is separated by sheets of "gun metal" glass with a subtle reflective coating

71 Proportion and scale

Scale and proportion are elements that are seen as top priorities by all plastic arts in that they decide the existence of the sense of form. In decorative design, scale and proportion need to be kept in harmony with the decorated spatial environment. Only by meeting this prerequisite can the glamour of decorative design be truly embodied.

In this case, the style of the decorative elements is consistent with that of the whole architecture while retaining the spaciousness and proportion of classicism. The shape of the beam and the home furnishings convey the fresh and natural artistic temperament.

Project name: Seacrest Semi-Custom Residence **Completion date:** 2008 **Location:** Irvine, USA **Designer:** Robert Hidey Architects **Photographer:** Courtesy Robert Hidey Architects **Area:** 604 sqm

1. The home reflects the relaxing movement of its ocean views, revealing itself through measured moments more than obvious dramatic gestures

2. Carved or turned wood, red tiles and iron grilles - architectural elements borrowed from the Old World - enliven the home and enhance the living, dining, foyer and great rooms with casual elegance

3. This home boasts two kitchens, one open to the great room, and the other for additional catering

1. Seacrest is located on hills overlooking the Pacific in Newport Beach, California

2. This wise design simultaneously preserves the restrained and quiet nature of the facade, while allowing for a tower that begins from the private retreat of the master bedroom suite and ends in an intimate top-level room with panoramic views of the Pacific

1. Seacrest's calculated composition of elements results in a holistic plan that evokes a refined elegance, which stands the test of time
2. The master bathroom

72 The use of affixture

The use of affixture is the re-decoration technique applied for restricted interior surface, by which the interior environment can be made more abundant and individualised.

In this case, the designer builds a magnetic wall running through all storeys. All family members can post their favourite pictures on their respective floors. In this way, the storeys are arranged in an organic organisation.

Project name: Kenig Residence **Completion date:** 2008 **Location:** New York, USA **Designer:** Slade Architecture **Photographer:** Jordi Miralles **Area:** 300 sqm

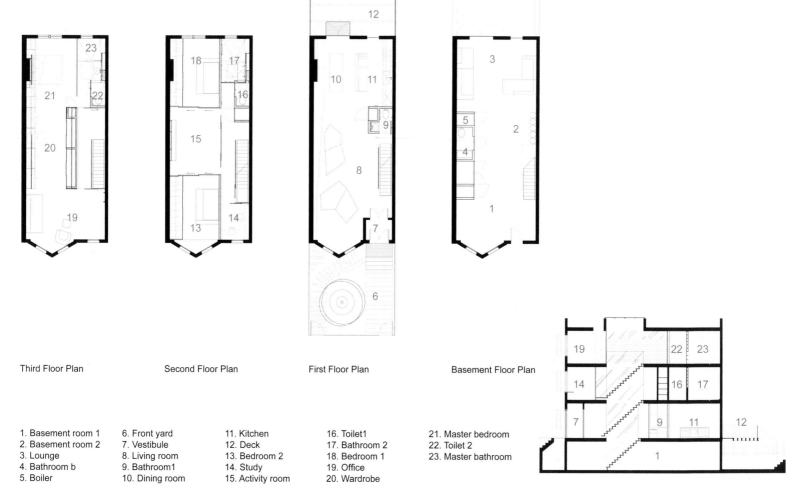

Third Floor Plan   Second Floor Plan   First Floor Plan   Basement Floor Plan

1. Basement room 1	6. Front yard	11. Kitchen
2. Basement room 2	7. Vestibule	12. Deck
3. Lounge	8. Living room	13. Bedroom 2
4. Bathroom b	9. Bathroom1	14. Study
5. Boiler	10. Dining room	15. Activity room

16. Toilet1	21. Master bedroom
17. Bathroom 2	22. Toilet 2
18. Bedroom 1	23. Master bathroom
19. Office	
20. Wardrobe	

Section Plan

1. Client was interested in creating a modern haven for his family, in a beautiful Brooklyn brownstone: a place that offered private retreat spaces as well as open mixing spaces to spend time together

2. The first floor level was opened up to become a loft-like living room and kitchen with an exterior wood deck floating outside, over the backyard. The flexibility of the magnet wall fosters the creation of zones organically, as people affix items of interest to them at their own floor-alternately the entire stair could be rigorously curated. Designer felt that the flexibility of the display wall mechanism was appropriate particularly for a family so rooted in a retail tradition

3. In the kitchen, the colour palette is focused on black and silver. Countertops are Absolute Black granite with a laminate on upper cabinets and island that features an abstract aluminium pattern on a black background. Mid level cabinets and security doors are aluminium sheet, with a custom pattern of circles and ovals that creates an optical illusion that the sheet is bowed out when in fact it is entirely flat

1. The second floor became the girls' floor with bedrooms, a study, kid-lounge and bath. This floor offers real flexibility as the rooms can be opened or closed with large sliding doors. In the open configuration, the entire floor is open like a loft space. By closing the doors, the girls can create a traditional closed bedroom space

2. The bathroom on this floor has a playful tile combination that mixes graphic tiles of a grass lawn with green glass cobbletones tiles

3. An extensive collection of rare shoes is featured prominently immediately adjacent to the stair entry on the floor, below the skylight. The "shoe wall" became an important personal expression as well as a unique decorative element

4. A new skylight was inserted into the roof, above the stair, accentuating the vertical rise and bringing natural light down into the home

5. Bachelor retreat was the idea of the third and top floor. There is a home office and extensive closet/dressing area as well as bedroom and bathroom

73 Suspension design

Suspension design is the second supplementation for the wall design. The arrangement of art works including oil paintings and photos can provide walls with a new visual sequence. Meanwhile, the articles used for suspension always possess some ornamental and collection value, endowing the interior space with some certain symbolic meaning.

In this case, the designer chooses the ceramic hanging dishes, photos and oil paintings as the suspension design elements of the walls. The collocation of these elements and other home furnishings give birth to the spatial ambience in the style of the eighteenth-century Britain.

Project name: Castel in the UK **Completion date:** 2006 **Location:** Oxfordshire, UK **Designer:** Alberto Pinto **Photographer:** Jacques Pépion **Area:** 3500 sqm

Perfectly symmetrical, it radiates out from the centre as a circle inscribed within a square. The four pronaos (entrance halls) and dome are reminiscent of Mereworth Castle, or, earlier in date, of Palladio's Rotonda near Vicenza

1. The eclecticism of the period allows for a freedom of action that eschews historicity and repetition

2. The interiors of the drawing rooms located on the first floor are not a reconstitution of the English eighteenth century, but a reincarnation

3. The family room is a prime example. In its glorification of the pleasures of the silver screen, it recalls that Tusmore House is a waking dream, the exultant recreation of England in an era of heroism

1. In the century of the English Enlightenment, in the "age of connoisseurs"-that of avid collectors, of great aristocratic families who governed vast empires of trade, industry, and agriculture, and for the present, with one of the great and the good. Periods overlap and often merge in the palace revolution at Tusmore House, the largest such edifice to be built in England since the end of the nineteenth century

2. The English eighteenth century allows ample space to more up-to-date concerns

3. For its interior, the designer bases his vocabulary on the grammar of its architecture, for the classical idiom is a language of which he has total command

1. Its plan is modelled on that of the great mansions that were created during the Hanoverian dynasty. The house's imposing silhouette towers like a monument

2. Each room exalts its colour and its spirit-ranging from the melting blue that dusts the Wedgwood cameos to a sunkissed yellow, one after another the rooms partake of a different atmosphere, each devised to match a given hour of the day

74 Paving design

Paving is the second supplementation to the basic design. In the interior design a main emphasis is the various carpets including hand-tied ones, woven ones, needled and tufted ones. They enrich the whole spatial configuration as well as enhance the visual richness of some areas.

In this case, the architects have created a space inside of an old building, taking into consideration the clients' exclusive accessoires and furnishings.

Project name: Private Apartment Berlin Friedenau **Completion date:** 2009 **Location:** Berlin, Germany **Designer:** Andreas Thiele Architekten **Photographer:** Hiepler, Brunier **Area:** 200 sqm

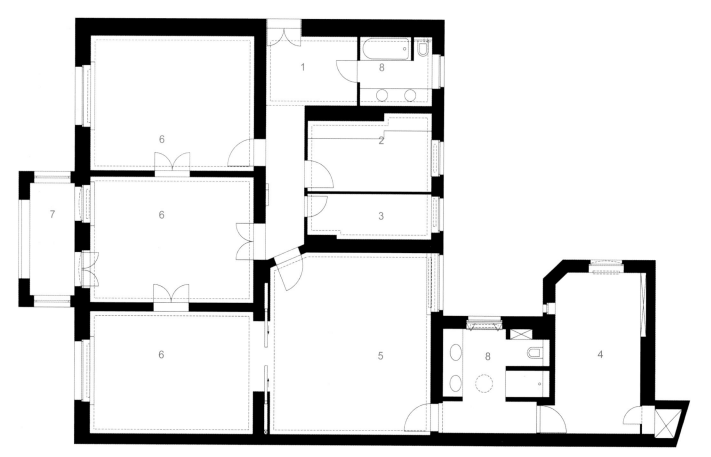

Master Plan

1. Entrance
2. Kitchen
3. Storage
4. Study
5. Bedroom
6. Living room
7. Loggia
8. Bathroom

The subtle changes and renovation of the rooms create a neutral and elegant backdrop which the clients had visualised for their personal furnishing. A specific challenge of this project was satisfying the individual requirements of the clients and re-creating the charm of this spacious old building

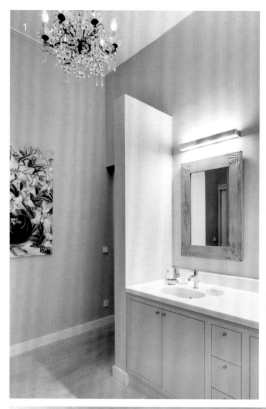

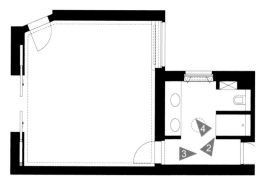

Bedroom Plan

1. The floor consists of white pigmented oak floorboards
2. The shower partition wall was cladded with large format white Thassos marble. In order to harmonise with the walls, the new built-in customised furniture was painted in the same colour
3. As the bathroom also functions as a walk-through room, the design aimed at emphasising a warm, comfortable quality
4. The bathroom window was fitted with custom-made interior window shutters with moveable wooden venetian blinds that function as a screen as well as an atmospheric element

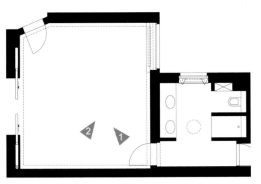

Bedroom Plan

1. The details of the old building fabric were restored and carefully accentuated
2. New wooden heating covers based on classical examples were installed

75 Furniture arrangement

As the main content of home interior design, furniture arrangement can not only demonstrate its own functions but establish the tone of home furnishings. From the viewpoint of human engineering, home furnishings, as the link of communication between men and the space in the interior environment, makes the empty room more comfortable and closer to life.

In this case, the designer places a seven-metre-long coach in the living room, which is convenient to admire the exterior landscape. Moreover, the modest styling showcases the elegance and dignity of the interior spatial ambience.

Project name: MC House **Completion date:** 2010 **Location:** Curitiba, Brazil **Designer:** Studio Guilherme Torres **Photographer:** MCA Estúdio **Area:** 600 sqm

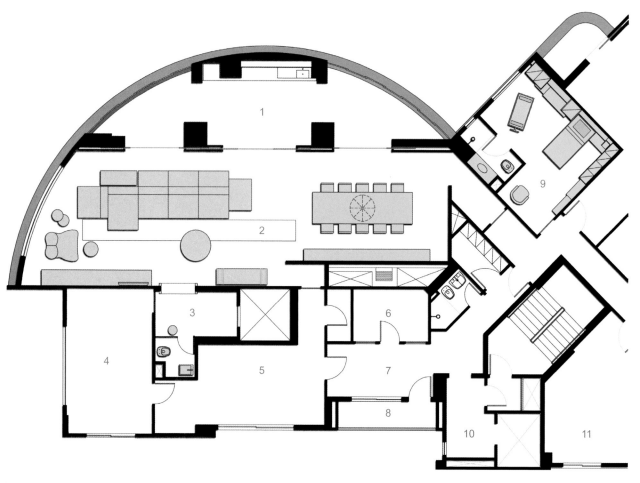

Master Plan

1. Gourmet	5. Kitchen	9. Baby room
2. Living room	6. Pantry room	10. Service hall
3. Hall	7. Laundry	11. Bedroom
4. Home theatre	8. Balcony	

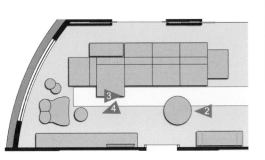

Living Room Plan

1. The hall was designed as a box covered with macassar ebony

2. In the rectangular space, travertine marble and macassar ebony were used as a timeless base to receive the design furniture

3. The property of 600 square metres had a social area with limited circulation and weak illumination. The architect proposed to eliminate walls aiming to create a wide and luminous living room. The living room was divided by a seven-metre-long sofa, that allows sitting on both sides. That was the alternative to enjoy the privileged view of a municipal park a few hundred metres away

4. The whole furniture line follows an unassuming style, inspired in the 1970s

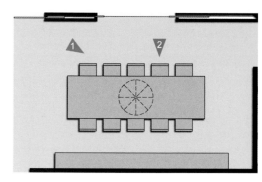

Dining Room Plan

1. The 1950s' dinner table was designed by the architect and it translates his contemporary spirit for this proposal

2. The matt stone wall contrasts with the mirror top dinner table sharply

3. The property, a typical apartment of the 1980s, was literally put down and rebuilt from scratch. All partitions that limited the rooms were removed. The toilets and two bedrooms were kept for structural reasons

4. The complicated picture frame and the wall lamp contrast sharply with the simple atmosphere

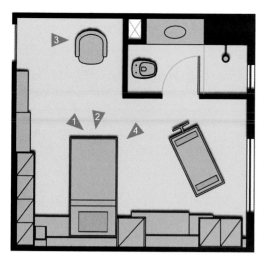

Baby Room Plan

1. Some windows were also eliminated, to create the concept of a box in which the ilumination plus wall and floor coverings would create a three-dimensional effect, like in a night club

2. The furniture in blue and white colour has unified the space's composition

3. Besides the scenographic effect, the illumination presents a great energy saving combined with a high luminous efficiency

4. The furniture in blue and white colour individually designed by the designer becomes the main decoration of the wall

76 The choice of lighting shape

As the main decorative elements of the home interior space, the lamps and lanterns often include pendant lamps, ceiling lamps, wall lamps, floor lamps, table lamps and the like, among which the pendant lamps in large scale can always be the independent decorative element of the space and moreover adjust the spatial height of vision.

In this case, to match up with the characteristics of different space ambiences, the designer chooses lamps in various shapes which not only offer lighting and illumination but become the necessary decorative elements of the space.

Project name: 40 Beverly Park **Completion date:** 2010 **Location:** Los Angeles, USA **Designer:** Landry Design Group **Photographer:** Erhard Pfeiffer **Area:** 2,323 sqm

1. With careful consideration to the home's orientation, the design allows for abundant natural light to enter every space and enables the concepts of passive solar and thermal mass to work well

2. The lights of the chandelier and wall lamp have formed a perfect reflective illumination effect, enhancing the level sense of the whole space

3. This estate takes advantage of modern building technologies while holding true to the design characteristics that make a chateau of France's Loire Valley so intriguing

1. The designer interpretes the classical interior style of the old buinding in a brand new way

2. By combining new concepts from both a design and environmental standpoint, the home set in its deeply rooted historical precedents has been propelled into the present day

3. The down lamps at the top ceiling have formed a strong sense of order

4. The arrangement of the chandelier has well balanced the sense of voidness, and meanwhile added the space with a sense of luxury

5. The down lamps and wall lamps in the bathroom only play the role of decoration, and the main light comes from the outside

6. The open lightings at the top ceiling have made the whole space bright and open

77 Direct illumination

In the lighting design of the home interior space, direct illumination means the lighting system that above ninety percent lights cast directly on the objects. The lighting system features centralised illumination and high brightness. In terms of the range of application, it is suitable for large-area or regional illumination task.

In this case, the lighting plan and layout for this project was a significant feature of the project and it was designed specifically around the client's evolving art collection and furniture layout. Like a museum, ninety percent of the ceiling lighting works directly with the art, objects and spaces to highlight those elements. The recessed ceiling lighting system allows great flexibility and as the art collection changes, the lighting plan can also be altered and changed to reflect the new art. Differing lamps can be added or subtracted to alter the light produced to feature or emphasise specific pieces. The entire lighting system is dimmable and programmable so that the mood of the lighting can reflect the time of day, season of the year or a public event.

Project name: Scholl 2 **Completion date:** 2009 **Location:** Aspen , Colorado, USA **Designer:** Studio B Architects **Photographer:** Aspen Architectural Photography **Area:** 666 sqm

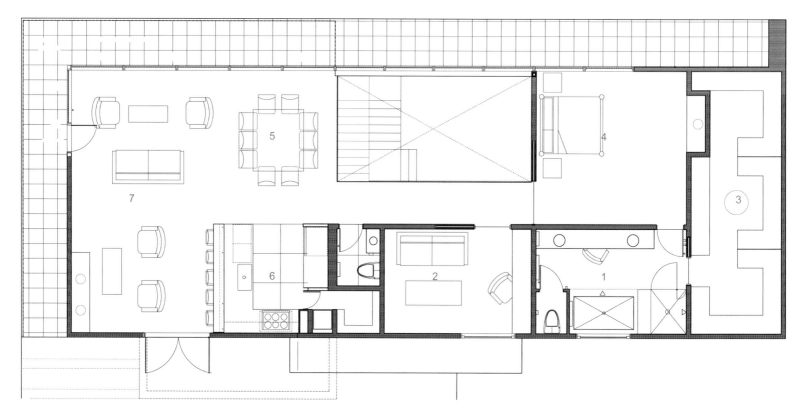

Third Floor Plan

1. Bath room
2. Office
3. Closet
4. Master bedroom
5. Dining
6. Kitchen
7. Living

Office+Dining+Kitchen+Living Plan

1. The upper social level is filled with natural light, gallery space, art walls and opens to a viewing balcony and private garden with access to a roof terrace via a cantilevered steel stair

2. Double height entry with stair detail and art

3. Interior shot of the living, dining and stair railing detail in early evening

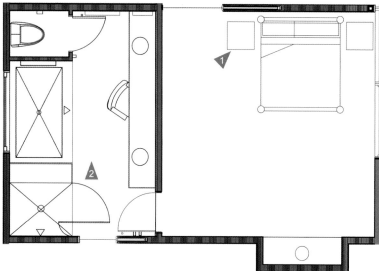

Master Bedroom+Bath Room Plan

78 Indirect illumination

In the lighting design of the home interior space, indirect illumination, also called reflected illumination, is an illumination system in which lights are first casted on a fixed interface and then rebounded to the irradiated objects. The illumination system features soft lights with unconspicuous drop shadows, which is suitable for the elegant and tranquil interior space.

In this case, the designer improves the sense of hierarchy of the open interior space through the application of the indirect lighting system which also enriches the artistic conception of the space.

Project name: The House of Cesar, Roberta and Simone Micheli **Completion date:** 2010 **Location:** Florence, Italy **Designer:** Simone Micheli Architect **Photographer:** Juergen Eheim **Area:** 200 sqm

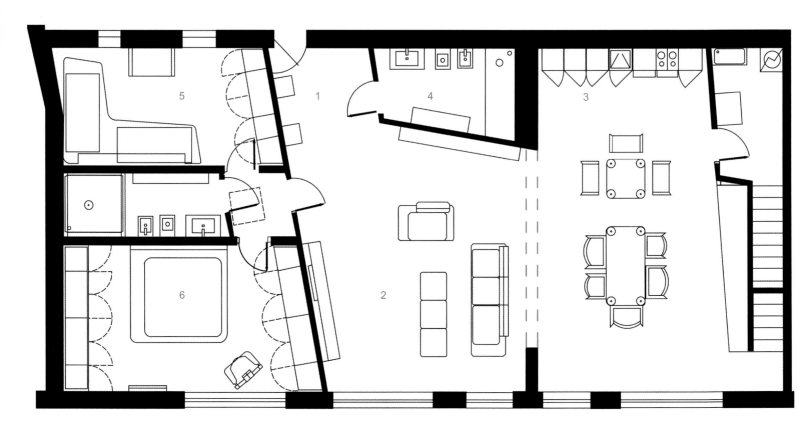

Master Plan

1. Entrance
2. Living room
3. Kitchen
4. Bathroom
5. Children room
6. Bedroom

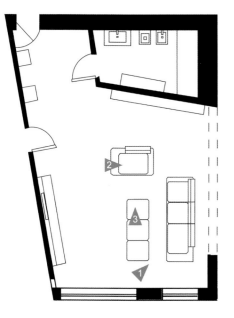

Living Room+Bathroom Plan

1. Walking on the staircase there is a space for children to play marking the end of the whole visual description pattern

2. In this way the full-height space which breaks the residential distribution rules is divided by a big brick arch; it features an unconventional distribution pattern on the ceiling and large openings revealing the opposite garden. The bookcase, an acid green highlight, the mirror furniture and couches, which look as soft as pink clouds, as well as the back wall lend liveliness to the overall architecture

3. The big size enamelled grès porcelain tiles floor are absolute white; they are as bright as the walls, the surreal ecoleather spherical poufs and the kitchen lacquering, the mirror furniture side surfaces and the bases of the stuffed furniture

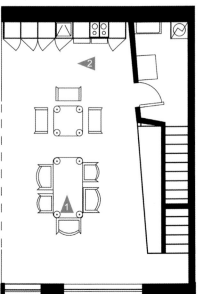

Kitchen Plan

1. All along this transversal dilatation glass tables for lunch and work are located together with a screen coming down the ceiling which can visually separate the kitchen from the rest of the environment. This informal crystalline, naive, immaculate, antibourgeois, suspended between minimalism and radical chic is torn by ringing and vivid patches of colours

2. The longitudinal axis which is triggered by the volumetric development of the living room meets a counterpoint, a minor transept in correspondance with the kitchen, a snow white sculpture marked exclusively by the partition of the doors which forms a niche in the added body resulting in dilating space in the dimension perpendicular to the windows

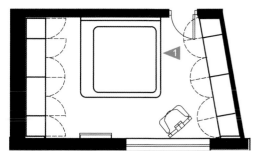

Bedroom Plan

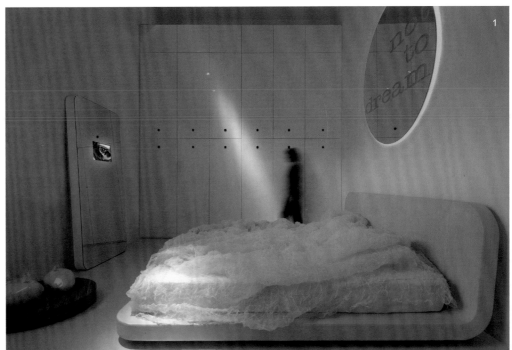

1. This house originated from the mould of a lively, dynamic, metropolitan future-oriented soul. It is a contemporary, intriguing, unpredictable mould which has the unmistakable signature of Architect Simone Micheli forged

2/3. The perception of this space is highly unconventional, visionary where colour bubbles flotating in a spotless sea generate emotions connected with childish innocence, lightness and joy

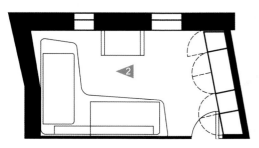

Children Room Plan

79 Diffuse illumination

In the lighting design of the home interior space, diffuse illumination means that the lights are diffused equably from around the light source, and then go through the semitransparent material which keeps out the lights to some extent so as to form the lighting effects. This lighting system features soft and stable lights, so it is applied to many sites.

In this case, the designer combines various kinds of lighting systems, among which the translucent marble is chosen as the top facing of the light source in the cellar, thus enriching the space dimension of the interior space by blocking the lights.

Project name: House of Mister R **Completion date:** 2009 **Location:** Moscow, Russia **Designer:** Za Bor Architects **Photographer:** Zinur Razutdinov, Peter Zaytsev **Area:** 560 sqm

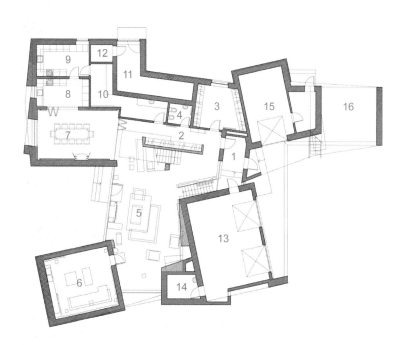

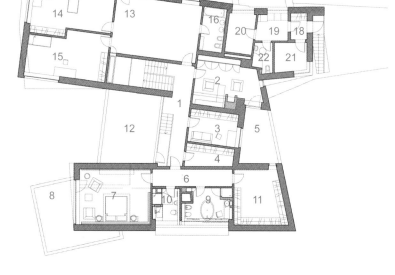

First Floor Plan

Second Floor Plan

1. Vestibule	7. Dining room	13. Garage for two cars
2. Entry	8. Master's kitchen	14. Storage
3. Walk-in closet	9. Service kitchen	15. Garage for one car
4. WC	10. Utility room	16. Car wash and storage
5. Living room	11. Boiler room	
6. Home theatre	12. Servant room	

1. Entry	7. Master's bedroom	13. Children playground	19. Staff kitch
2. Master's office	8. Balcony	14. Children room	20. Staff room
3. Nurse's room	9. Bathroom	15. Children room	21. Guard roo
4. Storage	10. WC	16. Bathroom	22. WC
5. Loggia	11. Dressing room	17. Balcony	
6. Bedroom's entry	12. Accessible roof area	18. Ante-room	

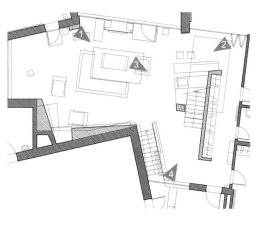

Living Room Plan

1. Almost the whole first floor is designed in white: light marble, grey river pebbles, glass and steel of the scarce fitments are here and there diluted with black built-in furniture constructed right on the spot

2. Bar counter which is constructively connected with the volume of the supporting column and stairs

3. The owner's part of the project is divided into public and private areas, which is emphasised by means of materials and colours

4. The geometrically complex bar counter which is constructively connected with the volume of the supporting column and stairs, is placed right in front of the steps leading to the second floor. While the original bench, serving also as stairs fencing in the other part of the living room, points at the downstairs leading to the "cosmic" wine cellar

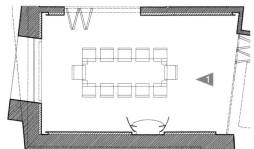

Dining Room Plan

1. In the dining room designers used the method for "cosmic effect" creation, but without mirrors: the sophisticated walls plastic makes you feel as if you're in the future in a kind of spaceship especially when you turn on the complex backlight

2. The customer wanted to see the outer space in the wine cellar, something vivid and extraordinary. But that area was quite chamber in fact. That's why designer wrapped it up in a wide strand of Corian and lit it. At the ends the designer placed stained glass mirrors. Designers intend to expand the space using this technique

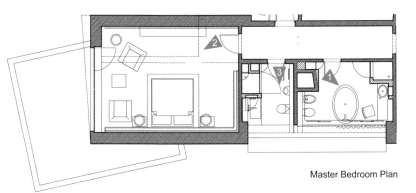

Master Bedroom Plan

1. Even the dark wenge panels and bathroom furniture don't break the idyll and visual peace

2. The second floor is more conservative and contrasts with the public zones. It was reflected in a more humane materials and colours choice: the oak floor, the pastel textile, the arm-chairs covered in textile create a calm home atmosphere in the interior

3. Above the bedroom you can see the sky through one of the zenith windows

80 Mixed illumination

In home interior space design, mixed illumination refers to the lighting system that integrates various kinds of lamps and luminous lighting system which creates the interior spatial ambience by the combination of several lighting systems rather than emphasising some certain kind of lighting effect.

In this case, the designer retransforms the old space by means of spatial reconstruction, material organisation and the arrangement of furniture and mixed lighting, thus endowing the interior space with warm and modern ambience.

Project name: Chet Bakerstraat **Completion date:** 2008 **Location:** Amsterdam, The Netherlands **Designer:** Hofman Dujardin Architects **Photographer:** Matthijs van Roon **Area:** 120 sqm

Master Plan

1. Hall
2. Kitchen
3. Dining
4. Living room
5. Terrace
6. Bedroom
7. Bathroom
8. Toilet

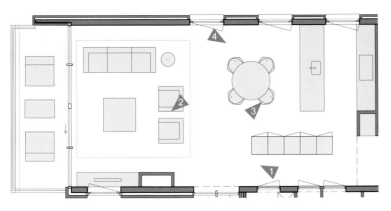

Kitchen+Dining+Living Room Plan

1. Entrance area with a view to the kitchen

2. Kitchen with a view to the entrance

3. The entire house is outfitted with mostly white and neutral colours. The kitchen is integrated in the living room. The large furniture creates intimacy and visual connections between the spaces

4. The apartment has been fully renovated with a new space planning, materialisation, furniture and lightning

1/2. The under-lights underneath the bath and closet illuminate the floor with a futuristic sentiment

3. The light colours and natural finishing give off a warm and modern atmosphere

4. The most excessive spatial changes made to the existing space can be found at the corners of the building

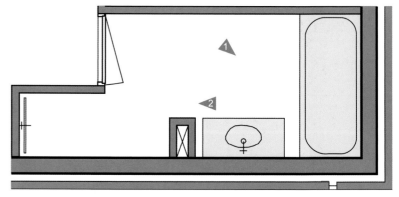

Bathroom Plan

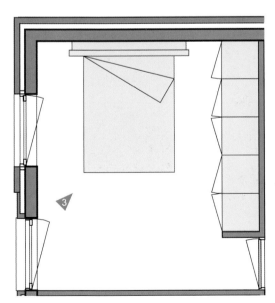

Bedroom Plan

81 Greening design

In home interior space, greening design means to achieve the transition and circulation between the interior and exterior space by introducing plants into the interior space so as to fulfill the interior environment with the elements of the exterior natural space. The geometric modelling of the modern architecture looks stiff and cold, while the interior greening design can change people's general impression of the space. The curves and soft feeling of the plants can provide people with a pleasant sense of scale and intimacy.

In this case, the designer infiltrates the exterior landscape and the interior space into each other through the transparent French window with the help of greening design, which not only heightens the sense of openness and the degrees of changes, but extends and enlarges the limited interior space.

Project name: Fish House **Completion date:** 2009 **Location:** Singapore **Designer:** Guz Architects **Photographer:** Patrick Bingham Hall **Area:** 726 sqm

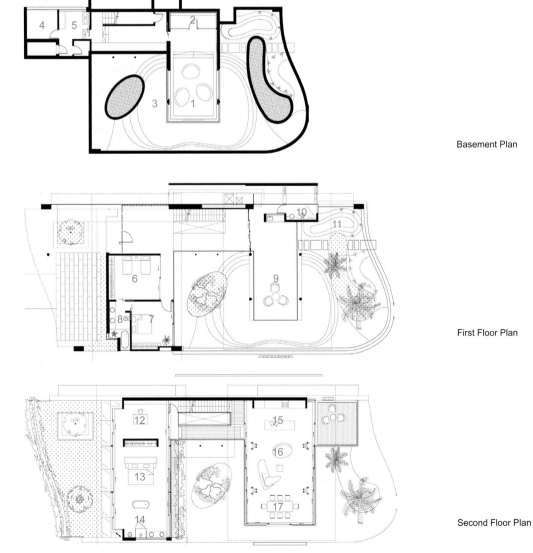

Basement Plan

First Floor Plan

Second Floor Plan

1. Media room
2. Wine cellar
3. Swimming pool
4. Store
5. Laundry
6. Bedroom
7. Guestroom
8. Bath
9. Verandah
10. Powder room
11. Jacuzzi
12. Study room
13. Master bedroom
14. Master bathroom
15. Kitchen
16. Living room
17. Dining room

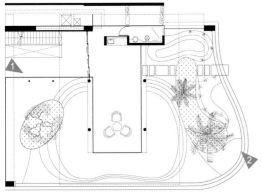

Verandah+Powder Room+Jacuzzi Plan

1. The house that is in the centre of the project is spiritualised by water and plants that surround the pavilion and give the impression of the real nature in every bit of the house

2. The designers managed to show a combination of technology, careful planning and sensitive design

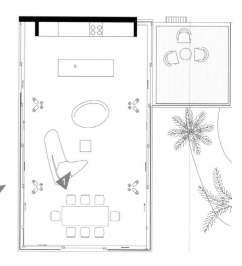

Kitchen+Living Room+Dining Room Plan

1. This modern tropical bungalow encapsulates the essence of living in the hot and humid climate of Singapore by creating open spaces which encourage natural ventilation and offer residents views to the ocean

2. The main design concept is to create a house which has close relationship with nature and this is achieved by having a swimming-pool linking the house with the landscape and ultimately visual connections with the sea

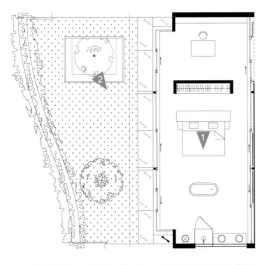

Study Room+Master Bedroom+Master Bathroom Plan

1. Fish House is a modest and yet luxurious residential design which gives residents opportunities to live in harmony and comfortably with nature

2. The main idea of designer was to create the hi-tech house close to nature

82 Furnishings for daily use

Home interior design may always encounter a large number of articles for daily use such as the home appliances, dinnerware, wine sets, stationery and books. These articles cannot perform the decorative function and sometimes it's inconvenient to use them, while the disadvantage can be offset and the decorative effects can be magnified if they are hanged or placed in order on the walls, the cabinet frames and the tables.

In this case, the designer arranges the daily commodities in an orderly way so that they are not only convenient to use but improve the sense of sequence of the space.

Project name: Minto 775 King West - 2-Bedroom Suite **Completion date:** 2010 **Location:** Toronto, Canada **Designer:** II BY IV Design **Photographer:** David Whittaker **Area:** 93-139 sqm

1. Set the table for an intimate dinner, or relax in the living room and enjoy the views from the floor-to-ceiling windows
2. The design created the perfect happy place with a modern aesthetic and exceptional use of space
3. In the kitchen, stainless steel appliances blend seamlessly with granite countertops and glass mosaic-tile backsplash

1. Expansive glazing that bathes the suites in light during the day and dazzling city lights by night
2. Marble countertops with elegant touches in the bathroom

1/2. Lively melange of pop art and bright colour in the bedroom

83 Art furnishings

In home interior space, the artworks, serving as ornaments themselves, are the last but the most important link of the interior space design. In the interior space, not all artworks are suitable for the specific environment and it has nothing to do with the quantity. They should be chosen according to the whole spatial scale and ambience. Usually, the standard is set centring on the visual comfortableness, for instance, the paintings and photography works on the wall and the sculptures and artwares on the table.

In this case, the designer not only effectively defines various functional areas through the arrangement of the artworks but coordinates the relationship of colour composition with the help of the colour suggestion of artworks.

Project name: Apartment in Kaunas **Completion date:** 2008 **Location:** Kaunas, Lithuania **Designer:** Indra Marcinkeviciene **Photographer:** Valdas Racyla (Valdas Račyla), Karlas **Area:** 92.38 sqm

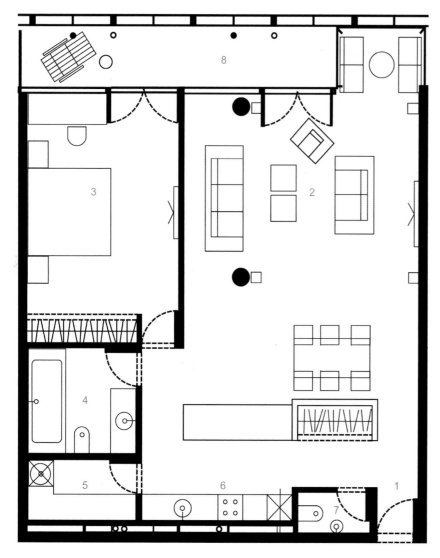

Master Plan

1. Hall
2. Sitting room
3. Room
4. Bathroom
5. Pantry
6. Kitchen
7. WC
8. Balcony

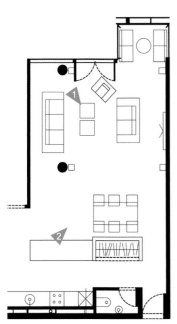

Hall+Sitting Room+Kitchen+WC Plan

1. The primary object in this interior is a painting, Seated Boy, by a famous painter, Vilmantas Marcinkevicius. It gives the conception of the colours which infuse in the whole apartment. Bright blue and turquoise is repeated in details. An extravagant stripy rectangle appears on the wall in the sitting room zone. The painting is highlighted in a decorative gilded frame designed by Loreta Svaikauskiene

2. All white walls and the water-resistant dark oak floor all over the apartment, give a strong background for other artworks, colourful furniture and various materials and fabrics

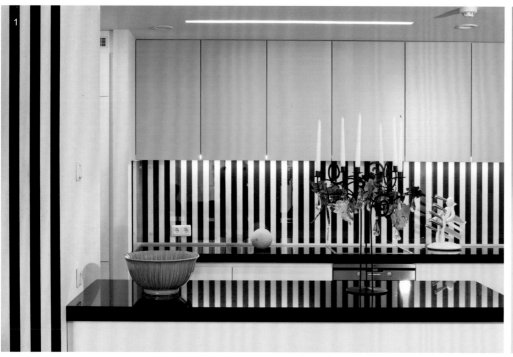

1. In the dining area and on the kitchen wall a rhythm of black and white stripes appears

2/3. The stripy wallpaper is covered with a glass for practical purposes. The same composition of colours and contrast prevails in the bedroom and the bathroom. It looks as if the chairs around the dinner table have been collected from Vilmantas's painting. Contrasts prevail in furniture, for instance, the yellowish green doors of the cupboards are of different shades and together create an impression of a concave shape

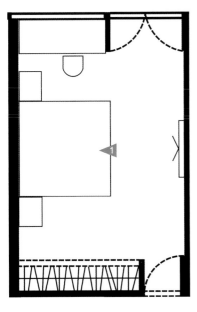

Room Plan

1. The warm light green in the bedroom is defused with white dots and softened with velvet textures

2. An openwork woodcarving by another Lithuanian artist Marius Jonutis is used for wardrobe. In the night time, a white and elegant wardrobe gives a soft intimate light towards the room, creating cosiness

3. The designer also likes using mirrors, which create light and mysterious reflections. They are everywhere: in the dining room, the living room, the bathroom. They are responsible for creating a slightly mystical atmosphere

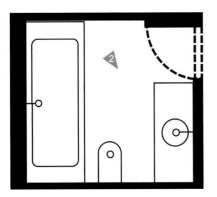

Bathroom Plan

84 Textile furnishings

In home interior space design, the fabrics, with rich colours, soft texture and remarkable decorative characteristics, are combined based on the practical applicability, comfortableness and artistic quality of the interior space.

In this case, the designer, in consideration of the fact that the client is an artist, effectively highlights the richness and abundance of colour in the collocation of the furnishing articles so as to give expression to the subtle emotion of the artist.

Project name: Family Residence in Vilnius **Completion date:** 2006 **Location:** Kaunas, Lithuania **Designer:** Indra Marcinkeviciene **Photographer:** Valdas Racyla (Valdas Račyla) **Area:** 254.28 sqm

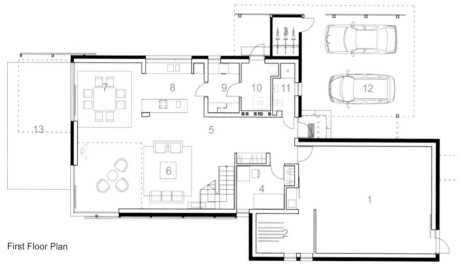

First Floor Plan

1. Painter's studio
2. Storage
3. Outside store room
4. Home office
5. Coridor
6. Living room
7. Dining room
8. Kitchen
9. Kitchen storage
10. Boiler room
11. Bathroom
12. Shed
13. Terrace

Second Floor Plan

1. Staircase
2. Bedroom
3. Bathroom
4. Master bathroom
5. Cloakroom
6. Master beddroom
7. Bedroom

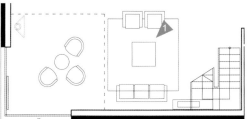

Living Room Plan

1. The fabric furnishings have coordinated the colours of the whole space

2. Bright colour, low-purity fabric furnishings become the decorated focus of the space

1/2. The owner of the residence is an artist. Light space and colours dominate here

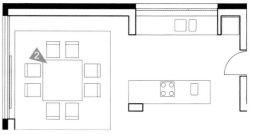

Kitchen+Dining Room Plan

1. The colourful fabrics play important role in the decoration of the space, giving the whole space a strong sense of order 2/3. The green fabric furnishings have highlighted the space's simplicity and elegance

85 Waterscape design

In home interior design, waterscape decoration, as a special category, imports the exterior natural elements to the interior space so as to increase the visual pleasure while regulating the regional climate of the interior space, activating the spatial functions of the interior space.

In this case, the designer creates a special recreational area for the interior space by combining the waterscape decoration with the swimming pool modelling.

Project name: Residence Malibu **Completion date:** 2009 **Location:** São Paulo, Brazil **Designer:** Fernanda Marques Arquitetos Associados **Photographer:** Rômulo Fialdini **Area:** 800 sqm

1. Entrance hall
2. Dining/ living room
3. Balcony
4. Kitchen
5. Lounge
6. Solarium

First Floor Plan

1. Fireplace
2. Fitness
3. Closet
4. Master suite
5. Suite

Second Floor Plan

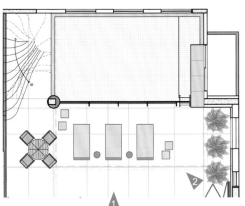

Solarium Plan

1. For the external terrace, the client proposed an automated retractable glazed metallic roof, so as to enhance natural daylight, during the day, even when closed

2. One of the main challenges in the project, a swimming-pool also in clear glass, had numerous superstructure studies carried out, in order to calculate the increased load on the slab created by the huge structure

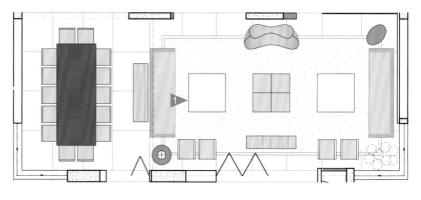

Dining/ Living Room Plan

1. Moving away from the obvious, coming up with innovative solutions and making full use of technology, each piece on it had to be unique and yet relate to the whole at the same time

2. Designer decided to concentrate the social area of the apartment on the lower floor, creating the maximum integration among the spaces. In line with the project, design chose large pieces, which have straight lines and are extremely contemporary. Besides the leather, velvet, metal and glass prevail in the rooms

3. The staircase and elevator to the top floor were proposed to be done in clear glass, in order to be integrated to the living room

4. Pieces acquired in auctions in New York stand out in the spaces, such as the curved stainless steel sofa designed by Ron Arad

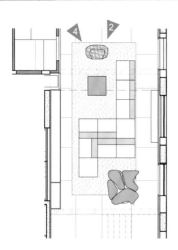

Lounge Plan

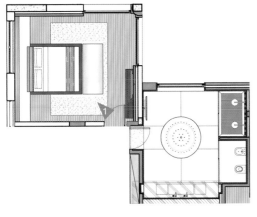

Master Suite Plan

1. The master bedroom was placed so as to look out to the pool

2. All lighting systems are dimmer-controlled and have lighting moods programmed into the automation system

86 Scene creation

In home interior design, decorative design is a process in which the designer makes the optimal choice and allocation of the articles in the interior space. As the sublimate of the interior design, it is also a process when idealisation and abstraction transform into life. Only by undergoing the step of decorative design can the home interior space truly demonstrate its individuality and be closer to the real life.

In this case, the designer creates a customised and comfortable ambience through the choices of the furniture in the living room, the plants in the corridor and the sculpture in the bathroom.

Project name: First Floor Penthouse **Completion date:** 2009 **Location:** Tel Aviv, Israel **Designer:** Z-A Studio **Photographer:** Assaf Pinchuk **Area:** 160 sqm

Master Plan

1. Entrance
2. Living room
3. Kitchen
4. Dining room
5. Bedroom
6. Bath room

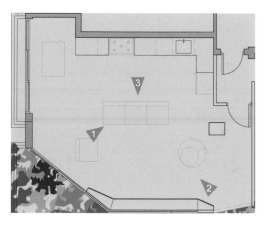

Entrance+Living Room+Kitchen+Dining Room Plan

1. This project ties to a broader interest in the distinction between public and private in residential spaces. If you follow the typology of living spaces you can see that one major thing did change in a way that everyone takes for granted now – the open public space of the living, dining and kitchen areas. This project examines the limits of this configuration which designers have inherited from the "loft" concept of the 1970s

2. Behaviours and lifestyles that shape the residential environment are very difficult to reshape. Designers tend to be very attached to spaces they grew up in and the things they know and feel comfortable

3. Conceptually designers were thinking of it as a flipped penthouse or courtyard, where instead of letting in the light, air and landscape penetrate from above, it is now carving through the apartment from its side. This inverted courtyard separates between public and private and creates an effect that removes the private sections of the apartment beyond an outdoor space as if they are two separate houses

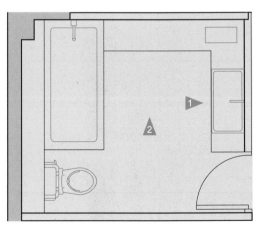

Bath Room Plan

1. The bedroom extends the ephemeral relations between inside and outside
2. The concept of the artificial landscape was carried through to shape the wall elevations and plans
3. The primary asset of the apartment is funnelled in, creating a horizontal courtyard. This funneled landscape separates public
from private, turning the bedrooms into a remote entity, when viewed from the open public space

DESIGN PRINCIPLES OF SPECIAL AREAS

87 Vestibule design

The vestibule is the beginning of the home interior space and also the starting point of the integration between man and the total environment. In addition to offering the basic functions such as serving as the ornaments, dressing space and the storage function, the vestibule is designed in the same style to that of the whole interior space. The design of the vestibule should focus on its simplicity, functionality and artistic quality. Meanwhile, the space subdivision of the vestibule influences the sense of scale of the whole interior space.

In this case, the designer builds a feature wall resembling a sculpture at the vestibule. The top of the feature wall has clear directivity. The abstract artworks in modern style at the entrance imply the style of the whole interior space.

Project name: Sutton Place Residence **Completion date:** 2008 **Location:** Midtown, New York City, USA **Designer:** Hariri & Hariri **Photographer:** Paul Warchol **Area:** 465 sqm

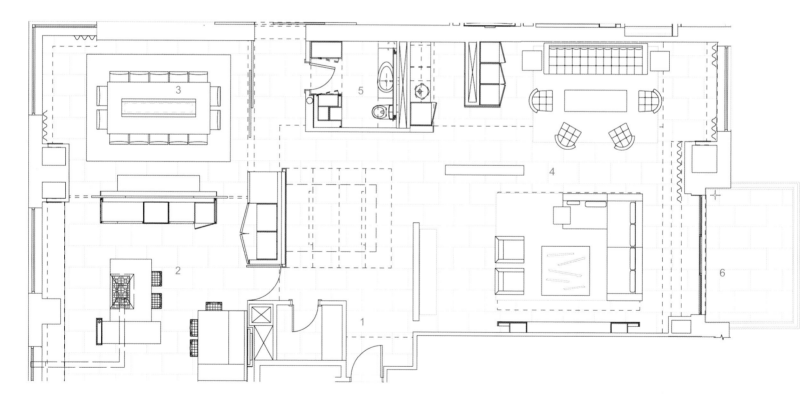

Master Plan

1. Entry
2. Kitchen
3. Dining room
4. Living room
5. Powder room
6. Terrace

1. A rectangular entry gallery exhibiting a sculptural-wall in dark wood embraces the visitors

2. An art-wall exhibits a mural by Julian Opie and a translucent glass wall brings natural light into the entry area. This material composition continues throughout the apartment creating a special continuity and visual connectivity

3. The flexible design of the partition wall at the entrance both as the part of the art exhibition hall and the beginning of the public area

88 Living room design

In home interior design, the living room, as the interior public area with the highest rate of utilisation, is arranged mainly in consideration of its function of entertainment, recreation, guest receiving and learning. The design principle of the living room is to rationally and effectually separate the main functional areas from the passageway so that they can not intersect or exert influences upon each other.

In this case, the designer links the living room and the exterior landscape, the terrace and the outdoor swimming pool together, which makes the living room more transparent and gives it more openness. The parallelism between the roof shape and the carpet gives birth to the centrosymmetric relationship of space configuration.

Project name: 27 East Sussex Lane **Completion date:** 2009 **Location:** Singapore City, Singapore **Designer:** Maria Arango, Diego Molina **Photographer:** Derek Swalwell, Courtesy of ONG&ONG Pte Ltd **Area:** 572.84 sqm

1. The living room connects to the swimming pool via a verandah which is constructed using the same stone as the facade. This ensures a consistent design language

2. With the low-pitched roof and the different tactile materials selected, the house is a delightful place to relax in

3. The spaces between outdoor and indoor are inter-connected so that a true resort home feel can be experienced

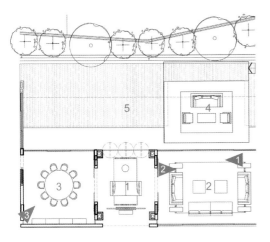

First Floor Plan

1. Forecourt
2. Living room
3. Dining room
4. Patio
5. Swimming pool

89 Study room design

The study room has become an independent space in new home space in that people still like losing themselves in the pleasure of reading though they can enjoy the convenience brought by the internet in the information era. During the designing process, such furnishings in appropriate scales as the bookshelves, ottomans, tea tables, blankets and sofas can all be chosen to increase the comfort of the study room.

In this chapter, both the two study rooms witness the careful arrangement of the interior furniture, the lamp styling and the lighting system. The cosy and comfortable interior environment is produced simultaneously in both of the two rooms through the creation of the spatial ambience.

Project name: Apartment No.10 **Completion date:** 2010 **Location:** Chengdu, China **Designer:** MoHen Design International **Photographer:** MoHen Design International

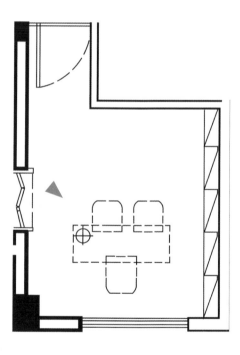

Study Room Plan

Project name: Villa No.12 **Completion date:** 2010 **Location:** Shanghai, China **Designer:** Hank M.Chao /MoHen Design International **Photographer:** Maoder Chou **Area:** 330 sqm **Main materials:** cherry wood finishes, French white marble, oxidation magnesium plate, stainless steel plated black titanium, iron board grilled white paint, mosaic parquet, cork flooring, matt cherry flooring

The desktop in the study room integrates with the independent space, creating a perfect reading environment. The cork floor has added the room a sense of warmth

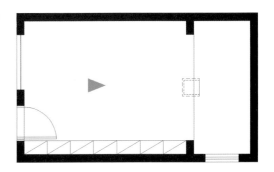

Study Room Plan

90 Kitchen design

For a long time, kitchens, as the central areas of the traditional family life, exist as a kind of auxiliary spatial form. Nowadays, however, the function of the kitchen is developing towards diversified direction. The kitchen space can be made to bring delight and enjoyment to people through matched kitchen facilities.

In this case, the designer connects the kitchen with the natural landscape and the outdoor swimming pool, which makes people intoxicated in the pleasure of cooking while increasing the visual joyfulness.

Project name: Vienna Way Residence **Completion date:** 2007 **Location:** California, USA **Designer:** Marmol Radziner **Photographer:** Joe Fletcher **Area:** 418 sqm **Award name:** Sunset-AIA Western Home Awards Custom Home Award

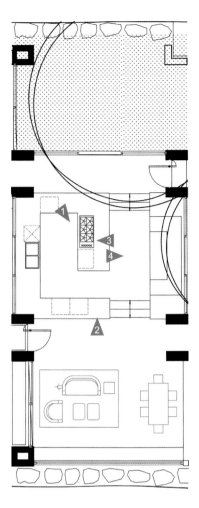

Kitchen Plan

1. The Vienna Way Residence, designed for a young family, is located on a large, extensively landscaped lot in Venice, CA. Floor-to-ceiling glazing and outdoor living spaces fully integrate the home within the California native landscape

2. The kitchen continues in the backyard's riparian landscape planted with rushes, reeds, and sycamore trees. These plantings give way to a large play yard filled with buffalo grass and surrounded by Oak trees and other California native plants

3. In addition to bridging the two main volumes, the kitchen is the centre of a water-related area that starts in front with a swimming pool and flows through the kitchen and over its green roof

4. The kitchen acts as the hub of the residence, connecting the public and private areas and providing views of the pool, side yard and rear property

91 Master bathroom design

The whole design style and form of the main bathroom should express the clients' pursuit of life quality and provide the clients with a private interior environment. Besides the basic function of bathing and rinsing, the main bathroom needed to be created within a comfortable spatial ambience through the layout, the material combination, the collocation of lights and the like.

In this chapter, the unique features of master bathroom are fully expressed through the functional partition, material combination as well as the collocation of lights.

Project name: Acqua Villa **Completion date:** 2010 **Location:** Texas, USA **Designer:** Winn Wittman **Photographer:** Coles Hairston

1. The collision of the open space and small-scale veneer material highlights the delicate atmosphere of space
2. The highly reflective materials make the overall space be more transparent and open

Project name: PIK House-ESPERTA **Completion date:** 2009 **Location:** Pantai Indah Kapuk, Indonesia **Designer:** Erwanto & Yettie **Photographer:** Harry Dee

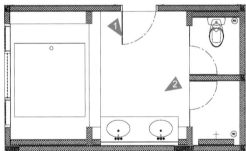

Bathroom Plan

1. Designer wants to give homey, comfortable and luxurious design not only for the host, but also for the guest or relatives
2. Collaboration of the architect and owner in the design of the space, contributes a good atmosphere and space with lighting design

Project name: Casa Son Vida **Completion date:** 2009 **Location:** Palma de Mallorca, Spain **Designer:** Marcel Wanders Studio **Photographer:** Gaelle Le Boulicault & Marcel Wanders Studio

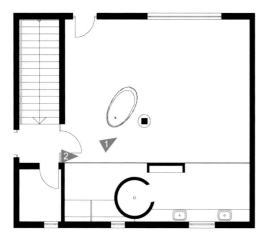

Master Bedroom Plan

1. The luxury residence transgresses the constraints of site and context, redefining luxury architecture as it is typified by the traditional and prolific Mediterranean and Tuscan styles

2. The home will capture the attention of the international design world with its sophistication and vitality, making a new destination for those in search of design exploration and inspiration

92 Terrace design

As the transitional area between the interior space and the exterior natural landscape, the terrace with a broad view, can bring people luxuriant visual enjoyment. The terrace can perform the functions of providing relaxation, catering, recreation and the like. As for the lighting design, it always combines the two lighting systems of natural lighting and accent lighting.

In this chapter, the terraces in two totally different styles convey the two ways of modernism and classicalism to interpret the open space, while they are the same in grasping the space configuration and understanding to the life.

Project name: Private Residence Sixteen **Completion date:** 2008 **Location:** Eagle Bay, Western Australia **Designer:** Dane Richardson **Photographer:** James Stati Photography

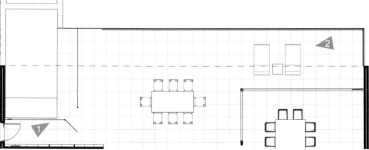

Terrace Plan

1. The owners were quite specific about connecting the main living space with the views and creating an easy circulation from the kitchen to the main entertaining balcony

2. The kitchen, living area and dining room flowed onto the main balcony and pool area

Project name: Town Classic **Completion date:** 2008 **Location:** Athens, Greece **Designer:** Cadena Design Group **Photographer:** Vangelis Rokkas

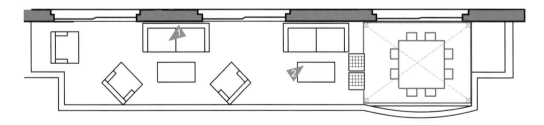

Terrace Plan

1. The orderly home furnishings' arrangement has taken full advantage of the balcony space
2. The colour and the texture have injected the balcony a sense of warmth and elegance

93 Attic design

The challenge of attic design is how to arrange the sloping roof and utilise the natural lighting. The varied top shapes and storey heights of the attic make it easy to form a flexible space sequence relation.

In this case, the designer reasonably and effectively sets up the public and the private space types according to the locations of the sloping roof and the window, guaranteeing the unity and coherence of the interior space by coordinating the material and the lighting system.

Project name: ATTICO **Completion date:** 2007 **Location:** Cuneo, Italy **Designer:** Damilano Studio Architects **Photographer:** Andrea Martiradonna **Area:** 240 sqm

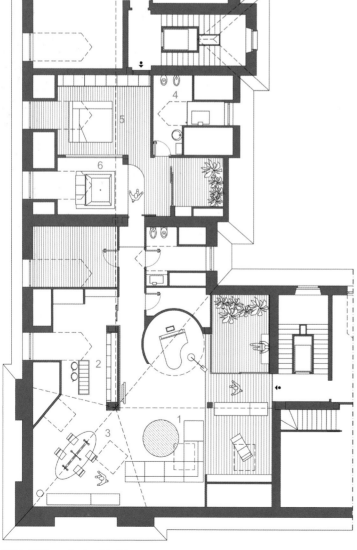

Master Plan

1. Living room
2. Kitchen
3. Dining room
4. Toilet
5. Bedroom
6. Bathroom

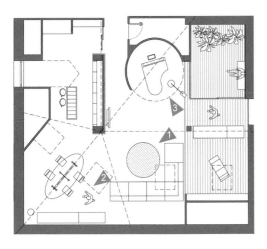

Living Room Plan

1. Converting this kind of apartments can be quite difficult because the attics have very little room at the roof's ridge and require customised spaces. Designer took the challenge, managing to create large rooms with few dividing walls, to give more breath to the apartment

2. The final result of the conversation is a bright, spacious and dynamic apartment that perfectly reflects the owner's needs

3. The chosen colours and materials help giving breath to the spaces and the white reflective floors create homogeneous surfaces next to parts made the chestnut wood and facing in Indian stone

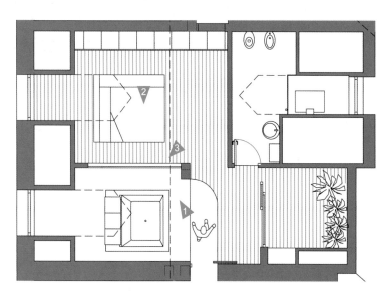

Bedroom+Bathroom Plan

1. The bed and the bathtub, separated by a glass, create two spaces for the wellbeing in communication with each other and the soft light dampens the rigid geometry of the room
2. The sleeping area is designed as an independent area, an alcove where to retire at the end of the day
3. The bathroom is the only closed room, where the shower is obtained at the cockloft level to exploit its height

94 Children's room design

Children's room is the space with the most flexible layout in home interior design. With the growth of children, the interior layout needs to undergo constant adjustments. The greatest feature of children's room is demonstrated in the colour scheme: the colour scheme with high saturation and low purity can provide children with a tranquil and calm mood while invigorating the interior spatial ambience. In terms of the furnishings, toys and other soft decorative articles are always the best choices which can not only create the childlike interior ambience but provide the children with protection.

In this chapter, the design of the children's room in each of the three different cases conveys the same design concept whether in terms of the colour scheme, the selection of the material as well as the arrangement of the toys. The interior space is full of child interests with the application of these unique design techniques.

Project name: 45 Faber Park **Completion date:** 2008
Location: Singapore City, Singapore **Designer:** ONG&ONG
Pte Ltd **Photographer:** Derek Swalwell, Tim Nolan

Project name: Narrow House **Completion date:** 2010 **Location:** Barcelona, Spain **Designer:** Jordi Antonijoan Roset, Francesc Solé Durany

1. The bunk bed provides more imaginary sapce for children
2. The cartoon pattern wallpaper together with the various shapes of toys injects the room a sense of interest
3. The abstract sculpture plays important decorative role in animating the children's room, and the soft fabric gives the room a sense of warmth

Project name: 12+Alder **Completion date:** 2006 **Location:** Portland, Oregon **Designer:** Skylab Architect **Photographer:** Steve Cridland

95 Multimedia room design

The multimedia room can be combined with the living room or designed as an independent space in home interior. The plane layout of the multimedia room includes mainly the passageway, the film-watching area and the bar. The multimedia room imposes relatively high requirements for lighting, especially the arrangement of the auxiliary light source which could not ruin the interior atmosphere while maintaining the certain luminance and decoration.

In this chapter, different multimedia room designs in the five cases all make perfect explanation of the shape selection of the lights, the arrangement of the light sources, the style of the furniture in the watching area and the colour scheme of the interior space.

Project name: The China Alleyway Memories **Completion date:** 2008 **Location:** Wuxi, China **Designer:** Maoder Chou **Photographer:** MoHen Design International/Maoder Chou **Materials:** marble, rust metal, walnut, titanium coating steel, coconut mosaic tiles, magnesium oxide board, oak handscraped flooring

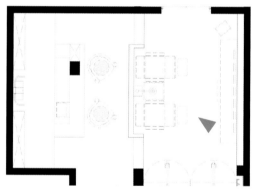

Media Room Plan

Lighting acts a crucial factor in traditional Chinese architecture, and it is also the part from the last space that does not properly expressed. In Chinese style building, the use of light effect is not just about pouring in the space, but it should be used with more hidden, little modest or even shy to pour on the space people need. It is little bit like the personality or nationality of Chinese people, connotation. This kind of natural light effect is able to give special feeling to the Chinese building. The branches of the tree are waving in the alleyway, along with the scene of children playing, combine with an old grandpa holding a long hookah, it was the image in the traditional triangle garden. The multi-function hall in basement, made with two rusted pivot door as entrance, the purpose of it is as a transition of space. This multi-function hall is the recreational place for watching a movie or taste a glass of wine from the wine collection. There is a corner in the hall which has a perfect outdoor view; when designer first saw this corner, he can feel every single pore of his body is stimulated. He set a huge potted plant in this corner with lot of exaltation.

1. The top black paint together with the reflective mirror makes the space calm and steady
2. The spotlights illumination has highlighted the prominent characteristic of the artwork

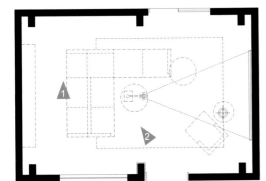

Media Room Plan

Project name: Villa No.12 **Completion date:** 2010 **Location:** Shanghai, China **Designer:** Hank M.Chao /MoHen Design International **Photographer:** Maoder Chou **Area:** 330 sqm **Main materials:** cherry wood finishes, French white marble, oxidation magnesium plate, stainless steel plated black titanium, iron board grilled white paint, mosaic parquet, cork flooring, matt cherry flooring

Project name: Acqua Villa **Completion date:** 2010
Location: Austin, Texas, USA **Designer:** Winn Wittman
Photographer: Coles Hairston

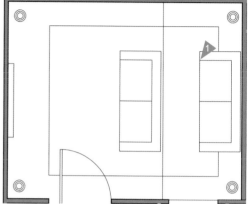

Media Room Plan

1. This home, and its organisation, palette of materials, unique decoration, and lighting are all a direct reflection of the client. It suits the client's passion for individual expression, and a place to play and relax

2. One of the main challenges faced by the architect was selecting furniture and decorative pieces that were contemporary in their looks yet were in keeping with the seaside mood

Project name: Laranjeiras Residence **Completion date:** 2009 **Location:** Rio de Janeiro, Brazil **Designer:** Fernanda Marques Arquitetos Associados **Photographer:** Demian Golovaty

Project name: Quidnet Road **Completion date:** 2009
Location: Nantucket Island, Massachusetts, USA **Designer:**
Kathleen Hay Designs **Photographer:** Jeffrey Allen
Photography

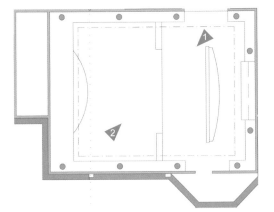

Media Room Plan

1. The design concept was to create a clean, simple, and unadorned summerhouse retreat that balanced sophistication with comfort
2. The challenge was that the house needed to serve not only as a comfortable haven for the family and their steady stream of houseguests, but also as an entertaining mecca for this jet-setting young couple

96 Reception room design

In home interior design, the reception room, with more flexible layout and more relaxed spatial ambience, embodies the clients' tastes, personalities and characteristics through the arrangement of furnishings.

In this case, the designer organises the material and the tone using the technique of minimalism, expressing the purity of the interior space through the collocation and contrast of white and black. The space of the reception room is enclosed by adopting the transparent glass partition wall across the entrance. Therefore, the public and the private spaces are made permeated and circulated to each other by using space design technique of relative division.

Project name: Transparent Loft **Completion date:** 2007 **Location:** Seattle, Washington, USA **Designer:** Jim Olson, Design Principal **Photographer:** Benjamin Benschneider

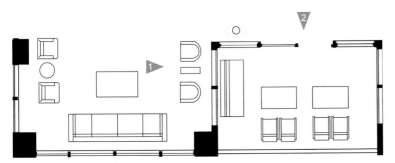

Reception Room Plan

1. The interior design is minimal in material and palette. A polished black floor sets off the glass and white walls, and is warmed by wood tables, panelling, casework and soft tones of upholstered seating, which are installed by interior designer

2. This eighteenth-floor condominium in downtown Seattle carries the idea of transparency to its logical extreme. The goal was to improve the boxy proportions of a speculative apartment, giving it the openness of a converted loft. The décor provides a neutral backdrop for the owners' collection of life-sized sculptural figures and minimalist paintings

97 Boxroom design

The boxroom, as a unique spatial form in home interior space, boasts the contents and forms designed in accordance with the clients' interests and hobbies. Sometimes, it is connected with other public areas to ensure the openness and negotiability while sometimes it exists in the form of the exhibition space. As a result, the relevant area of space should be left to be used as the passageway. In terms of some special collections, the special equipment needs to be installed to make sure the stable temperature, moisture and lights.

In this chapter, the boxroom design in each of the two different cases gives perfect explanations of the surface and the syntagmatic relations between the space surfaces in the corresponding space.

Project name: Mountain House **Completion date:** 2009 **Location:** Jalisco, Mexico **Designer:** Ricardo Agraz **Photographer:** Mito Covarrubias

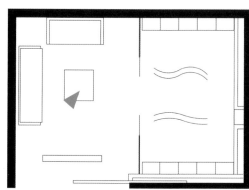

Boxroom Plan

Due to the programme features, the house hosts in its centre one of the family's most precious places: the wine cellar. Perfectly set within the mountain, it fulfills all the requirements to be so: controlled temperature, humidity and lighting, whereas it allows place for a wine bar and the capacity to add up to other public areas such as dining and living room by a retractile door piece

1. The lower level plan enjoys a high ceiling which houses a formal gallery, large wine cellar and provides two guest suites with an attached massage room
2. Detail of lower level stair into art gallery

Boxroom Plan

Project name: Scholl 2 **Completion date:** 2009 **Location:** Aspen, Colorado, USA **Designer:** Studio B Architects **Photographer:** Aspen Architectural Photography

98 Outdoor swimming pool design

As the extension of home interior design, the design of the outdoor swimming pool is the effective way in which people can keep intimate contacts with nature in a limited space. The outdoor swimming pool is always designed together with the terrace, the bathing area and the plants to jointly create a comfortable recreational ambience.

In this chapter, the outdoor swimming pool design in each of the two different cases becomes the visual focus in the living environment and effectively coordinates the relationship between the interior view and the exterior landscape.

Project name: Villa Amanzi **Completion date:** 2008 **Location:** Phuket, Thailand **Designer:** Original Vision **Photographer:** Marc Gerritsen

1. Cantilevered over a massage sala, the swimming pool completes the composition
2. It is the focal point that draws the eye to the view and instills a calmness that provides balance with the energy of the architecture

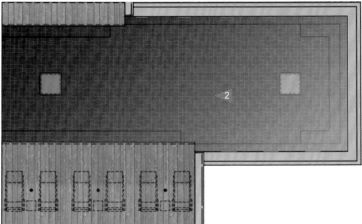

Pool Plan

1

Project name: Beira Residence Completion date: 2006 Location: Amparo, Brazil Designer: Marcelo Novaes Photographer: Gustavo Olmos

Pool Plan

1. The pool had to be set in a different level than the house but the integration was essential. It has an infinity edge that forms a waterfall on the level of the house. By this way if you are sitting at the house's terrace you immediately realise that there is a continuance of the garden above

2. This pool is very special because it holds the jacuzzi and an underwater sun deck

99 Roof garden design

With its own objective limitation in the integrated design of the home space, the roof garden, a special functional area, however, has won more and more attention from the designers and the clients, as people increasingly hope to enjoy the kindness of nature within reach along with the acceleration of the urbanisation.

In this chapter, the roof garden design in each of the three different cases effectively integrates the functional areas such as the recreational area and the dining area. A comfortable outdoor activity area is effectually created with the help of the collocation of the furnishings and the lights.

Project name: Le Bleu Deux Show Flat A **Completion date:** 2007 **Location:** Hong Kong, China **Designer:** PTang Studio Ltd **Photographer:** PTang Studio Ltd

1. The lighting has become the decorative element in the roof garden to connect different functional areas together

2. Pieces of classic furniture are scattered throughout the space to accentuate its neutral tone

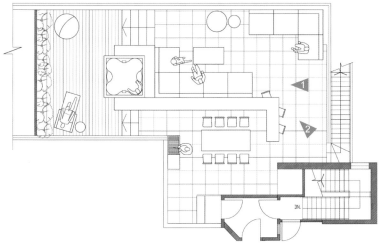

Roof Garden Plan

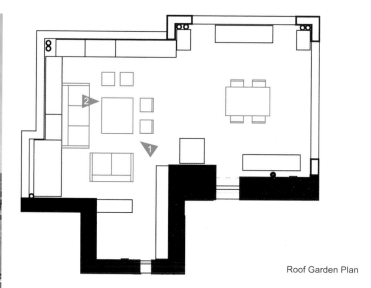

Roof Garden Plan

1. With the distant skyline, the roof graden look like a sanctuary in the bustling city
2. The blue tables and chairs echo with the blue sky, integrating the roof garden into the natural enviroment

Project name: Greenwich Village Penthouse **Completion date:** 2010 **Location:** New York City, USA **Designer:** SPG Architects **Photographer:** Daniel Levin

1. The orderly flooring makes the open roof garden be more compact

2. The roof garden with gazebo

Project name: PIK House-ESPERTA **Completion date:** 2009 **Location:** Pantai Indah Kapuk, Indonesia **Designer:** Erwanto & Yettie **Photographer:** Harry Dee

100 Courtyard design

In the design of villas, the courtyard design is the extension of the home space design. At the beginning of the design, the functional partitioning of the interior plane and that of the courtyard are carried out simultaneously. The passageway design connecting the interior and the exterior space in particular is the primary consideration. The courtyard design involves site planning, pavement design, greenery design, waterscape design and other structure design.

In this case, the courtyard design beautifully coordinates its relations with the villa building by putting up the ground pavement which deserves people's attention, the flower bed and the waterscape. The environment design of the courtyard endows the interior space of the villa with more openness and mobility.

Project name: Dillon Residence **Completion date:** 2006 **Location:** Scottsdale, USA **Designer:** Urban Earth Design **Photographer:** Bill Timmerman **Area:** 446 sqm **Award:** Crescordia Award for Environmental Excellence, the Valley Forward Association, AZASLA Award of Merit, 2008

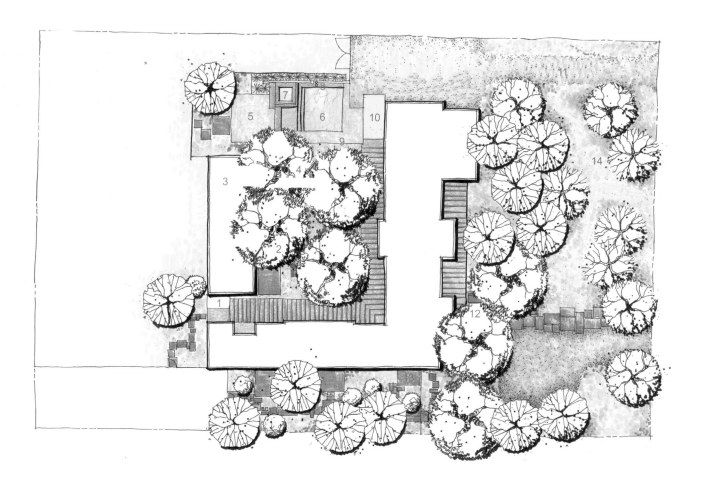

Master Plan

1. Zen garden	6. Pool	11. Decomposed granite drive
2. Turf panel & mesquite trees	7. Spa	12. Fountain
3. Master suite	8. Sheer decent waterfall	13. Patio pavers
4. Courtyard	9. Retractable fence	14. Native landscape
5. Pool deck	10. Outdoor kitchen	

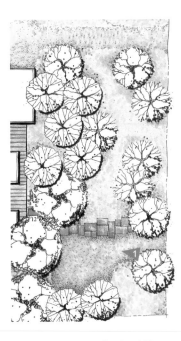

Courtyard Plan

1/2. Dwelling in the desert, celebrating the rich characters and qualities of the native landscapes of the southwest can be a challenge for homeowners in suburban settings who desire a contemporary lifestyle

Pool Plan

1. Employing effective design techniques that use drought tolerant and native materials with strong yet simple elements and the clean lines of modernism, this home exemplifies authentic regionalism in a Sonoran landscape setting

2. A neat square of turf in the courtyard creates an oasis and usuable space for parties, while keeping overall water use and maintenance low

3. The design challenge was to preserve the privacy that makes this area so valuable, while creating a functional and expressive landscape design

Index

51. Hyunjoon Yoo Architects

Contact: yoo@hyunjoonyoo.com

53. Archikubik

Contact: info@archikubik.com

54. HEAD Architecture

Contact: anna@headarchitecture.com

55. Janof Hald Architecture

Contact: amy@janofhald.com

57. O2 Architecture

Contact: info@o2architecture.com

58. BAKarquitectos

Contact: bakarquitectos@yahoo.com.ar

60/85/95. Fernanda Marques Arquitetos Associados

Contact: karen@fernandamarques.com.br

61/73. Alberto Pinto

Contact: contact@albertopinto.com

62. MONTAGNA LUNGA

Contact: info@montagnalunga.be

63. MGP Arquitecturay Urbanismo

Contact: felipe.gonzalez@mgp.com.co

64. Antonio Sofan

Contact: asofan@msn.com

65. SB Architects

Contact: hhebert@sb-architects.com

66/68. Kathryn Scott Design Studio

Contact: admin@kathrynscott.com

69. Taipei Base Design Center

Contact: tbdc@asia-bdc.com

70. JANSON GOLDSTEIN LLP

Contact: mj@jansongoldstein.com

71. Robert Hidey Architects

Contact: barbara_pressman@mac.com

74. Thiele Architekten

Contact: info@thielearchi.com

77/97. Studio B

Contact: studiob@sopris.net

78. SIMONE MICHELI ARCHITECT

Contact: staff47@simonemicheli.com

79. Za Bor Architects

Contact: zabor@zabor.net

80. Hofman Dujardin Architects

Contact: michiel@hofmandujardin.nl

81. Guz Architects

Contact: guz@guzarchitects.com

82. II BY IV Design

Contact: info@iibyiv.com

83/84. Indra Marcinkeviciene

Contact: indra@interjeraibesaiko.lt

86. Z-A Studio

Contact: info@Z-Astudio.com

87. Hariri & Hariri

Contact: mr@haririandhariri.com

90. Marmol Radziner

Contact: coralie@socialblueprint.com

91/95. Winn Wittman

Contact: ttlens@earthlink.net

91. Tec Architecture

Contact: julie@secretagentpr.com

91/99. Erwanto & Yettie

Contact: esperta@cbn.net.id

93. Damilano Studio Architects

Contact: d.damilano@gmail.com

94. Skylab Architect

Contact: amery@pushplusminus.com

95. Kathleen Hay Designs

Contact: info@kathleenhaydesigns.com

96. Blue Medium, Inc.

Contact: ozgur@bluemedium.com

97. Agraz Arquitectos

Contact: ana@agrazarquitectos.com

98. Marcelo Novaes

Contact: luciana@marcelonovaes.com

98. Original Vision

Contact: fiona@original-vision.com

99. Ptang Studio

Contact: rainbow@ptangstudio.com

100. Urban Earth Design

Contact: mdollin@urbanearthdesign.com

©2010 by Design Media Publishing Limited
This edition published in January 2012

Design Media Publishing Limited
20/F Manulife Tower
169 Electric Rd, North Point
Hong Kong
Tel: 00852-28672587
Fax: 00852-25050411
E-mail: Kevinchoy@designmediahk.com
www.designmediahk.com

Editing: Arthur GAO
English Translation: Li HE, Weinan DAI
Proofreading: Qian YIN
Design/Layout: Jie ZHOU

ISBN 978-988-15071-0-5

Printed in China